W9-AQN-049

Date Due

54629
Wuellner

Theodore Lownik Library
Illinois Benedictine College
Lisle, Illinois 60532

St. Procopius College Library
Lisle, Ill.

GRACES OF THE RISEN CHRIST

Theodore Lownik Library
Illinois Benedictine College
Lisle, Illinois 60532

Designs by Frank Kacmarcik

BERNARD WUELLNER, S.J.

GRACES
OF
THE
RISEN CHRIST

The Bruce Publishing Company
Milwaukee

Theodore Lownik Library
Illinois Benedictine College
Lisle, Illinois 60532

WITHDRAWN

IMPRIMI POTEST:

William J. Schmidt, S.J.
Praepositus Provincialis
Provinciae Chicagiensis, S.J.

NIHIL OBSTAT:

John A. Schulien, S.T.D.
Censor librorum

IMPRIMATUR:

✠ William E. Cousins
Archiepiscopus Milwauchiensis

die la Decembris, 1959

244
.242436
W95g

Library of Congress Catalog Card Number: 60–8242

© 1960 The Bruce Publishing Company
MADE IN THE UNITED STATES

54629

INTRODUCTION

Easter has many meanings for the mind and many joys
for the heart. Some of these are considered in the chapters of this book. The chief centers of attention are neither
the individual appearances of the risen Christ nor their
apologetic value as proving His godhead. Preference is
given to aspects of the new life in Christ and to thoughts
on the Christian Passover, as suggested by the liturgy.
These official prayers of the Church speak and sing of the
new life of the risen body, of the life of faith, the life of
grace given in baptism and renewed in penance, the life
of union with Christ in the Eucharist, the life of fervent
preparation for heaven, the life of God's people gathered
in Christ's mystical body, and the life of the world to
come. All these activities of our Christian existence merit
our prayerful pondering.

The episodes of our Lord's glorious life are conceived
to have occurred in approximately the following order.
Christ rose. He went at once to visit His Mother, as Chris-
tians commonly believe, though this event is not in the
Gospel record. During this visit the angels opened the
grave, and the guards fled. Jesus showed Himself to Mary
Magdalene; soon after to the holy women returning to
the city; then to Peter. In the late afternoon He joined
Cleophas and his companion on the dusty road to
Emmaus. That evening He appeared to the Apostles and
others gathered with them in Jerusalem. The following
Sunday He came again, with Thomas present. Then the

scene shifted to Galilee where the Master held a great
assembly with five hundred or more of His followers. Another morning He joined seven of them fishing on the
Lake of Tiberias and had a special conference with Peter.
Sometime James also enjoyed a private interview. Back
in Jerusalem He had a final feast and discussion with them
before going out to Olivet, whence He publicly ascended
in the sight of one hundred and twenty of His friends.
After ten more days, the promised Spirit came upon
Mary, the Apostles, and perhaps some others of their
company. A few years later, the risen Christ appeared to
Paul on the occasion of his conversion.[1]

The word *grace* is used in these pages to refer to any
divine blessing which is connected with the Resurrection
of our Saviour. The reader would do well to consult the
Easter Vigil ceremonies, the paschal and Pentecostal Mass
texts, and the offices of the whole Easter period to find
the perfect graces for which he should pray in union with
Christ and His Church.

When exact quotations from the New Testament are
given, the Kleist-Lilly version has been used.[2] The Douay
is used for the Old Testament.

May paschal peace fill every spirit that strives to rise
with Christ.

CONTENTS

GRACES OF THE RISEN CHRIST

1. THE GRACE OF THE RISEN BODY

This Easter dawn, when Christ the Morningstar[3] comes radiant from His grave, starts one of earth's perfect days.

Outside the tomb softly colored skies seem to be decked with legions of angels rising in shimmering rows and waiting to see the glory of their King when He will appear. Among them stand Michael, the angel of victory; Gabriel, the angel of the Incarnation; and Raphael, the angel of healing.

Looking down from the skies, they see the Lord's burial place, closed by a mighty stone and marked with official seals. They watch the guards patrolling back and forth in the surrounding garden. It is on this third day on which trouble would come if that buried Man's predictions had any weight, their officer had been told. These alert soldiers, however, think themselves ready for any challenge.

Within the dark tomb, the scarred and motionless corpse of Christ lies in its tight shroud and face cloths. Though dead, it is still God's body; for the second Person of God remains united to it. No decay has begun in it during the two nights and one day of its lonely repose in the vault that Joseph of Arimathea had provided.

Suddenly a bright band of angels comes into the locked tomb. After adoring, they remove the grave clothes, and robe the sacred body in fresh flowing raiment that looks like spun gold.

Then at the bidding of God and upon the Word's own command, the soul of Jesus flashes back from Limbo, enters the grave, and hovers awhile over the body, as though to impress upon itself the everlasting memory of this crucified figure. The soul re-enters its own body; it joins every cell; it rebuilds the whole human nature of Christ. The heart at once beats again; the nerves respond; the muscles grow supple. All welts, bruises, and dislocations are healed; calluses disappear from His carpenter's hands and traveler's feet; and all the marks of old sufferings vanish except for the five major wounds.

The fallen Christ stands again. He stretches out His arms in the sign of the triumphant cross. He speaks to the Father those grateful words which the Church puts into the Introit of the Easter Mass: "Father, I am risen and am still with You. Alleluia, alleluia, alleluia."[4] This is His Father's gift that answers His prayer at the Last

Supper to receive the glory which belonged to the Son before the world began.⁵

His quick mind organizes His thoughts for the busy day ahead of Him. He acknowledges the honors of the attending angels and instructs them about rolling back the stone for the coming party of mourning women, announcing the event to them, and guarding well the site and its souvenirs. Then He pierces the tomb's walls as easily as light moves through clear glass. Though the mobs have seen him die in shame, alone and unseen He issues from the tomb to living glory. Unnoticed, He slips through the net of pacing legionaries.

As soon as He is free and away, angels from the sky banks whirl down and roll the circular rock away from the front of the tomb. At the sonic boom of their coming, an earthquake shocks the garden; for this resurrection is a world-shaking wonder. The downrush of the heavenly spirits and the trembling of the ground dash the guards to the earth. A bit recovered, they see the wide-open grave and run in panic to their hirers.

THE GLORY OF HIS BODY

It will do us good devoutly to imagine the looks and actions of His risen body. During His previous life He had not let the fountain of gladness which His soul enjoyed in the vision of the Blessed Trinity show any marked effects in His flesh and sensory life. But today He lets the spirit's joy in seeing God flood through His body, sing in His human heart, and shine in His features. Once on Tabor three Apostles had glimpsed His glory when His transfigured countenance shone as the sun and His raiment had gleamed like fresh snow. Today He is even lovelier to behold than He was when transfigured on Mount

Tabor. His face, strong and lively and relaxed, speaks of assured victory. The eyes sparkle with glad love for God and men. His hands that forty hours ago twitched on the cross are calm and free. His unnailed feet support Him without effort as though the force of gravity had no influence on His body. He stands startlingly erect, seemingly ready to spring heavenward. His whole body speaks of immortal health and most vibrant life. All shadows of concern, all lines of anxiety, all expectations of sorrow, all strain of unfulfilled desires have left His majestic face. Every little feature and gesture tells us that all is well with Him.

The beauty of His body is entrancing; it is God's delight in a perfect physical object. His skin, as saints have seen it in visions, seems to have a special soft and youthful whiteness. The inner light of the soul seems to shine through it, like light gleaming through jeweled windows.[6] A sweet fragrance adorns Him, not a fading funereal odor to mask mortality, but something delicate and living, a heart-lifting perfume that adds a special enchantment to His radiant presence.

The five wounds tell us that this is the same body, vivified by the same soul, that recently hung bleeding on the cross. The same height, the same figure, the same features, the same tones of voice, the wounds in the same spots, and dozens of other identities between that crucified Man and this risen Man assure anyone who knew Him that despite amazing differences in these two states of His body, He is the same Jesus Christ.

This surprising fact happened on our earth and took place for our sakes. He loved us very deeply to allow His feet again to stand on this world which had bound Him to a cross, to let His smile fall again on men who had gloated at His agony, to let His voice be heard again by men who had shouted bitter curses at Him.

Theologians call our attention to other qualities besides the radiant beauty of His glorified body.[7] It is now a spiritualized body, sharing in a new way the characteristics of His spiritual soul and completely responsive to its control. Like the soul, the glorified body and its every cell can now never die. It cannot suffer or ever again be hurt, wounded, or dismembered. Christ's body can move as swiftly as the soul wishes it to go, leaping instantly, if the soul so orders, to some star at the rim of the universe. The sudden appearances of our Lord among His Apostles, without any opening of doors or windows, show that matter cannot confine it. It needs no food and no rest. Yet it is a true body of three dimensions, structured as a human body, visible, audible, touchable, resistant, warm, and sentient. These qualities will last permanently in His state of glory.

The First Fruits of the Dead

We join our chanted alleluias to the millions of congratulatory songs which honor our Lord in His joy, glory, and beauty. On this day which the Lord has made for rejoicing,[8] we are happy for His sake that He rose again on the third day as He said. We have reason to be glad for our own sakes, too, for He gave up His grave for us. His risen body vividly reminds us that His resurrection marks the end of the dominion of death over the children of Adam and begins the new empire of life for the children of God. "He is the head of his body, the Church, . . . the first to rise from the dead."[9] "He is the first fruits of those who have fallen asleep in death, because since man is the cause of death, so man is the cause of the resurrection from the dead. Just as in Adam all men die, so too in Christ all men are brought to life. But each in his own (turn): Christ the first fruits; then Christ's own, when he comes."[10]

Adam's corpse is the universal model of death for all men as infected by his sin. The new Adam's resurgent body is the pattern which all the just, redeemed by Him, must copy. He rose in the Easter springtime. In the golden harvest days the Son of Man will call all who have died in His grace to rise to a glory like His own. Some day a piercing, imperative trumpet, angel-powered, shall ring over all burial places on land and sea. The dead will leap up in answer; their souls will rejoin their bodies; their full humanity will dart forward to appear before the Judge of the living and the dead. The dry dust of millions of Christ's redeemed shall receive from Him the gift of immortal bodily life when their souls return from heaven to revive their flesh. Christ's own glory shall touch and perfect them in pure beauty. He shall transform them into the image of His own risen body because their souls are already conformed to His Passion, grace, virtues, and glory.[11] Angels might well envy our human likeness to Christ, King of Angels, on that day when we stand in new life before Him.

"With what kind of body will they come back?"

St. Paul answers:

> What is sown is perishable;
>   What is raised is imperishable.
> What is sown is sordid;
>   What is raised is glorious.[12]

After our moldering in the soil, deathless glory shall clothe us with a dignity that reveals how precious a creation of God human bodies are. Though less beautiful than Christ's, our bodies shall have the very same qualities which His displayed in the days after Easter: bodies exempt from pain; unable to become ill, decay, or die; more agile than light; penetrating matter at will; totally and forever perfect in life and form. The splendor of each shall be measured by the merit of each man. This rising is not like that of Lazarus who was destined to die again. Nor is it a rising as of invalid old folks from a hospital bed, still needing such helps as glasses, hearing aids, false teeth, crutches, and cosmetics. All the just shall appear in golden mature youth, unhelped by illusions created by hairdressers, jewelers, and tailors. Perhaps it will be the privilege of our guardian angels to garb our risen bodies for our appearance in the temple of God before the admiring eyes of our Saviour. "When Christ, your life, appears, then you shall appear with him in glory."[13]

Something like this is implied in our acts of faith. "I believe in Jesus Christ, who the third day rose from the dead. I believe in the resurrection of the body and life everlasting." I know that my Redeemer is alive and that I shall see Him — in His flesh — by the eyes of my glorified flesh.[14] He has promised this resurrection from the dead to those who believe in Him[15] and who in the days of their mortality receive His risen body in Holy Communion.[16]

Alleluia, then. He is risen as He said. Alleluia. We shall rise as He said.

2. THE GRACE OF HIS WOUNDS

The risen body of Christ returned bearing the five major wounds which it had received on the cross. We know this truth because Christ graciously met Thomas' demand to see the nail prints and put his fingers in them and lay his hand within the Lord's side. He appeared with the same wounds to St. Francis Assisi, St. Catherine of Siena, St. Margaret Mary, and a number of other stigmatics

8

Theologians agree that the Saviour keeps these wounds through all eternity in heaven.

All His other wounds have disappeared. The welts from the scourges, the bruises from the crosspieces, the gashes from the thorns, the skin swollen by the bloody sweat and cut by sundry blows are cured. Even the vessels enclosing the five remaining wound marks are healed, yet five depressions remain in the tissues as special openings in His glorious flesh. Far from disfiguring Him, these beautify Him the more where the precious blood shines through them, much as the blushing crimson of healthy lips adorns the human face.

Why did the Son of God retain these wounds? St. Thomas Aquinas gives five reasons, which summarize nearly all the likely purposes; for they explain what the wounds mean to Christ in glory, to His witnesses, to His Father, to the redeemed, and to His enemies.[18]

To begin with, the wounds add to the honor and splendor of Christ risen. Other heroes may be decorated by campaign ribbons, battle stars, or a distinguished Service Cross; but when their bodies fall to dust, they lose all evidence of their courage. In the body of the Hero of Calvary His exploits are inscribed forever. The marks of the nails and of the centurion's lance are a living memorial of His mighty fight. Outshining all other members of His body, these garnet badges record the wedding of His humanity to the cross on which divine love won a loveless world.

As His risen Body is the model of all other holy bodies that are to rise, it is likely that His perpetual wounds indicate that His heroes' glorified bodies may be honored by living souvenirs of their wounds borne for Christ. As baptism, confirmation, and orders mark the soul in the image of Christ's priesthood, so certain copies of Christ's cross-bearing may be forever fixed in the bodies of martyrs, penitents, soldiers fallen in battle, and injured firemen and police.

The sight of the saving wounds was certainly strong evidence of His identity for those to whom He appeared; and this is a second reason for preserving these marks. His Mother's eyes would instantly catch the contrast between His wounded form on Calvary and His glorified wounds. Magdalene clung to those immortal wounded feet on Easter morning. Peter, John, and James had seen Him months before transfigured on Thabor, but then He did not have these tokens of His sacrifice. Seeing and touching those warm, very real wounds won Thomas' complete assent to His resurrection. No one else could wear relics such as these. However amazing the fact that He is risen, yet this body cannot be anyone but He. The wounds make impossible any mistake about His identity.

Thirdly, the eternal paschal Victim is ever offering His wounds to His Father in our behalf, reminding His Father of His loving death on Calvary, and pleading in the language of these red scars that God would give us forgiveness and all the aids to holiness which we need to share in His Passion now and in His glory hereafter.

The same five wounds speak to us, the redeemed, of our Redeemer. They are gold-red tongues, telling us of His mercy and asking for our love. They shield, encourage, inspire, and invite us, in turn.

Since they are a victor's wounds, they protect the defenseless, guard the fearful, and keep the sinner in the fight. "Within Thy wounds hide me." This line from an old prayer expresses both the request of the devout for a resting place in these wounds and the petition of the penitent for a sheltering refuge.[19] These glorious wounds are not the dripping wounds which physicians must touch to heal. We, the ill, touch the divine Physician's wounds that their contact may cure us.

These wounds also encourage us. For their memory revives our confidence in Christ's great mercy to the contrite whom He purchased as His own by His streaming blood. Infinite generosity waits to reward those whose hope in Him honors these wounds.

They strongly inspire us to thank God that the bitter hours of Calvary are over and that the wounded Jesus has entered into glory. They call us to humility, for they remind us that our spiritual successes are won only when His supporting hands and brave heart assist us. They strengthen us to suffer with Him and for Him, and even to request that His wounds would shine in us, thereby to make us conformed to the pattern shown us on the Mount[20] and ready to rejoice when God considers us worthy to bear some pain for Christ.[21]

His hands, feet, and heart invite us to come close to Him with proffers of sympathy and deeds of reparation by which we may return some love to Him.[22] The wounds invite those suffering in mind and body to turn to Him for sympathy, refreshment, strength, and self-forgetfulness and to unite their wounded feelings and sorrowing hearts with His.

The fifth purpose of these permanent wounds will be seen when Christ comes in majesty to judge the living and the dead. They will be His credentials to judge human use of His redeeming gifts. In them the condemned will read the mercy offered and spurned; the just will read in them the good news that their names are listed in the book of life. The wounded Judge will infallibly know who have believed in and honored His holy wounds.

The Great Rose of Calvary

Looking on these dear wounds of our Saviour, we feel something of the wondering joy of Magdalene and Thomas when they touched them. With them we kiss them, one by one. Like John, who was allowed to lay his head on the Master's breast, we would lean, with His permission, on His glorified wounded breast. We understand why poets of faith have called these the five red-gold roses which bloomed on Calvary and remain forever fresh in heaven. We linger especially over the astonishing great Rose that reaches from His side up to the tip of His Heart.

This greatest wound somehow means more to us than all the others. This open heart speaks love's true language of sacrifice to our hearts. It insisted after His death, when still joined to His divinity, on giving forth all its blood and serum for us. Though its lancing was an unnecessary desecration of His dead body, yet it began that devotion to the Sacred Heart with which the Church has become aquiver because of our Lord's personal plea to St. Margaret Mary: Behold this Heart so deeply in love with men and so little loved by them.[23]

Genuine devotion to the Sacred Heart combines the tenderness and reverence, the sweet affection and vigorous action, the penitential grief and victorious love which are so hard to realize together in religious activity. The profound mystery of this Heart's love is imparted to each Christian especially in that moment when he consumes the glorified Heart in Holy Communion. At that moment we may welcome His wounds with Thomas' cry: "My Lord and my God." Loving adoration will delight in greeting Him as God of our hearts and Heart of our God.

His wounds given to us in the Eucharist remind us of

that gift of the martyr, St. Saturus. Drenched with blood from one bite of a leopard, he was being carried from the amphitheater, mortally wounded. Near an exit he passed Pudens, a soldier friend who was waiting his turn to combat for Christ. Saturus asked the soldier for his ring, plunged it into his own wound, and gave it back as a legacy of his love and as an incentive to courage.[24] Christ has done even more for us by giving us His very heart.

The Grace of the Open Heart

The open Heart of Christ bids us always keep our hearts open to the outpouring of His love and free to stream forth our love to others. The wounded Heart wishes His friends to practice His own sympathy for the suffering members of His mystical body. It is not enough to hail His wounds as great pledges of His love for us.[25] We must also by daily charity console Him wounded in His mystical body.

Of the many admiring prayers which we might address to the wounded Christ, one that deserves our attention occurs early in the Easter-vigil service while the priest is blessing the paschal candle. During the ceremony the minister inserts five red-waxed grains of incense into the center and four ends of a cross which has been scored on the ornamented face of the big candle. As he puts these grains representing the wounds into the candle that represents Christ, the celebrant prays: "Through His holy and glorious wounds may Christ the Lord keep and save us. Amen."

We may pray to Sts. Mary Magdalene and Thomas to help us win the privilege of touching His wounds one day in heaven. We may beg the Virgin Mother that, after our years of sharing Christ's wounds on earth, she would show them to us in all their glory in heaven. We may plead with the Saviour for one embrace of His Sacred Heart. The hope of one such embrace should ready us for any service that He requires on earth. Through all eternity we shall adore and bless the Christ because by His holy wounds He has redeemed the world.

3. THE GRACE OF A VISIT WITH MARY

RESURRECTION THROUGH A MOTHER'S EYES*

The dawn meeting of Jesus and Mary is a favorite memory
of the Catholic at Easter time. Though not recorded, even

* St. Ignatius Loyola in his *Spiritual Exercises* recommends that re-
treatants make a contemplation on the visit of Jesus to Mary on Easter
morning. The method of contemplation used here is the application of
the senses. We imagine ourselves to be privileged observers of this meeting; we use sight, hearing, touch, taste, smell; and we reflect devoutly
on our impressions. This method is difficult for those who are not at
the time deeply recollected or who are not highly imaginative. In regard
to the present subject, it may even be distasteful to those who prefer to
stress the divinity of the risen Christ and Mary's intimate unity of soul

15

in St. Luke's Marian Gospel, this appearance of Jesus fits well into the interval between Christ's rising and His revelation of Himself to the women returning from the empty tomb.

The first concern of the victorious Son is to see His Mother. He loves her most; she loves Him most. She deserves to see Him first as a reward for taking the greatest share in His Passion and in His loving offering of it. She needs Him most, for her wound is deeper than any other, not because of her lack of faith or hope in His resurrection, but because of the depth of her sympathy for Him on the cross. To her He will come, not to prove His resurrection but to share its joy with her. He is aware of her morning prayers which are calling for Him. Her requests had always been a law to Him. This is so again in His new life of glory.

On their way to anoint the body of the Lord, the three Marys have stopped at His Mother's residence to ask her if she wished to come along or send flowers or other tokens of affection to the tomb. She gives them her gentle no. The fathers and theologians have surmised that she did not accompany the women either because she had given her word to John and the Apostles that she would not risk her health by renewing her intense mourning of Friday afternoon or because she was too exhausted to walk that distance or because she knew that Jesus would be already

---

with this divinity. A reverent use of the imagination on the human relationships of the Son and His Mother has, however, much sanction in the customary processions of Spanish-speaking peoples on Easter morning who arrange a public meeting of a statue of the Virgin Mary and of the Blessed Sacrament. In literature, St. Teresa's vision, reported in her *Autobiography*, speaks of the Lord's long stay with His Mother because of her slow recovery from her grief. The famous Ludolf of Saxony's *Life of Christ* (II, chap. 70) and Mother Mary Loyola's meditation on the Resurrection in her *Hail! Full of Grace* make considerable use of the application of the senses.

risen by the time they reached the cemetery. The last supposition seems to be the best. She is sure that He will rise today, for He had plainly said so. She knows that He will come to her today, for she knows how He thinks and acts. But her stainless faith does not know at what time today He will come.

She is alone, eyes closed, heart withered by the recent horrors, valiantly yearning for His rising.

All of a sudden, without any announcement by Gabriel, her radiant Son stands in front of her. To His tender gaze she still looks like the sorrowful woman whom He had committed to John beneath the cross. Because of her deep sorrow and spent strength He knows He must be gradual in breaking to her the sight of His glory. He waits very quietly to catch her attention.

What first makes her aware of His presence in the room? Is it the ruby light beaming from His wounds? The magnetic fragrance issuing from His spiritualized body? The soft blowing of His breathing? After He has stood a while, unnoticed, near her, a little restlessness and curiosity seem to come upon her. She moves, looks up, turns her head toward her Son. She sees Him — all life, all beauty, all victory, all glory in one strong countenance! She hears the sonorous music of His voice:

"Mother!"

As He moves half a step closer to her, He speaks once more in His joyful tones and very slowly:

"Alleluia, Mother! I am just now risen, dear heart, and am come first to tell you."

Recognition, identification, wonder, joy, adoration, welcome, love, congratulation, praise, joy, burning interest in every detail about Him follow each other like the notes of a new soaring melody.

A world of happy beauty bursts in her eyes. Her face

blossoms in a greeting smile. The vision washes from her features all the pain-carved lines. His strong sensitive carpenter's fingers lift her up. Today He will not let her kneel to adore His divinity; today He would be her son and comforter, nothing more.

Drawn by His fingers, she comes to a standing position. He tilts her head, holds it in the cup of His hands, and bends to kiss her forehead. That comforting kiss breaks her tension and puts her soul at peace. She clasps His glorious wounded Heart to her own, while He removes the seven swords of her sorrowing. It is the happiest homecoming that has ever occurred. To Jesus, this is the sweetest and gladdest hour of this day. To her, it is the most wonderful moment of her life on earth. No other mother has yearned more for her son to come back from deadly battlefields than she has desired Him to return from the hill on which He died. The widow of Naim did not take to her heart her son risen from his bier as fondly as this holy Mother caresses her martyred Son.

That He is alive and sound and happy again is altogether sufficient to make her happy. She is so glad for His sake that she does not even think of her own delight.

What does one say when overpowered by joy? What does one say when one meets God in His glory? After many a wondering Oh! and Oh! she may have gasped His name:

"Jesus! Son!"

The intensity of her joy deepens His own Easter gladness. She tries to tell Him how she feels.

"Jesus, it is indeed Yourself. How wonderful You look!"

What admiring thoughts hurry across her mind as she appraises the changes in His physical form. The marvel of immortal health after so harsh a death. The splendor of His body, so soon after its descent into the dark earth.

The wonder of wounds that make perfect the flesh that bears them, the human flesh born of her.[26]

Being His mother, she notices the Easter robe with which the angels have clad Him and the kingly halo with which they have crowned Him. She catches the flame of beauty surrounding His Heart's wound. She reads in His eyes His special pride in this resurrection jewelry of His five wounds.

A Son's Paschal Gifts

Little by little, He lets His shining form grow brighter and brighter, now that she is used to Him, so that she may feast still more on His victory. As always when He came back to her, He has some special gifts and special news for her. Besides the gift of His human presence, He deepens her knowledge and love of the Blessed Trinity; for this is the greatest of all joys. He pours His Easter peace into her soul and raises her mind to perfect contentment with the provident decree of His Father that He should win men's souls by His bitter sufferings and death in her sight.

After a time, He gets her seated, and they fall to talking of their common memories and of His fresh plans. He speaks His filial thanks to her for her sympathy in His sufferings. He brings her a lovely message from her dear Joseph, whom He had seen in Limbo. He asks her whether there is any special favor He can do for her today.

"I have one big request," she replies. "Yesterday, each of Your Apostles visited me, and I promised each to pray for God's forgiveness for any disloyal fear of theirs, and I assured them that I would speak to You for them. But I do not think they understood what I meant about speaking to You again."

"Of course, Mother, that is granted. There is nothing

that I desire more than to forgive each of them. I will reassure them later today when I see them."

His face lights up and He laughs a little as He anticipates the merry moments when He makes Himself known to His old friends.

He left her, then, to go on His errands to His stricken friends, leaving these precious gifts in her rejoicing heart. This is her Easter, her Pasch, on which she has passed over from compassion to co-rejoicing. She knows that this has been the best of all His visits. In jubilant thanksgiving she hums and then sings her own *Magnificat*. When Magdalene, the Marys, and John burst in upon her with their news of the empty grave and the appearance of the Lord, they see from her star-studded eyes and her radiant recovery from her misery that they need not tell her. She knows, none better.

It will be one of the extra joys of heaven to have Mary herself tell us the full story of her Easter hour with Jesus.

Our Easter Call

To visit Mary is one of the privileges of believers in the Resurrection. In imitation of Jesus who called this day on His Mother, we ought to make a glad visit to her today. We try to make our congratulations on this day of her joy match our compassion for her on Good Friday. As we finger our way along the glorious mysteries of the rosary, we assure her of our filial joy because her dolors are ended and her glory with Jesus has begun.

We prefer to be among those of her children who come to her not only when they are in trouble and want something, but also when they are glad. We thank her for her part in the redemption and for being the Lady of Consolation to us. We have good news to tell her about ourselves, that we have risen from our sins, have scored some victories against ourselves, and met her Son in Holy Communion today. Whether we appear before the Lady altar or some picture of her, whether we come with a spring flower as a gift or in our spring attire as a special honor to her, she will welcome us. All we need to bring along is a loving heart. In any case she will be pleased to hear us join the whole Church in that exultant salute, the *Regina Caeli*, which takes the place of the Angelus during the Paschal season. Legend claims that angels in Rome first chanted its words centuries ago.[27]

> Queen of Heaven, rejoice. Alleluia!
> Because He to whom you gave noble birth — Alleluia!
> Has risen again, just as He said. Alleluia!
> Pray to God for us. Alleluia!
> Be happy, be glad, Virgin Mary, — Alleluia!
> For the Lord has indeed risen. Alleluia!

To this antiphonal hymn the priests' Office adds a lovely extra gift to Mary.

> O God, who judged it fitting to cause the world to rejoice by the Resurrection of Your Son, our Lord Jesus Christ, grant our request that through His Mother the Virgin Mary we may take hold of the joys of eternal life.

These everlasting joys surpass even the Easter joys, and Mary wishes us to share them with her. In her immaculate body, already risen and glorious, our Mother's joyous smile now rests on the glorified face, wounds, and heart of her Son. Her eyes of mercy are watching over us, her children, as we pass through this valley of tears.

Pray for us, Mother, in your peaceful heart which is waiting for us to come on an everlasting visit with you in heaven. After our exile, give us that entrancing smile which glowed on your face when you saw your Son on Easter morning.

4. THE GRACE OF THE PASCHAL LAMB

The lamb is a favorite artistic symbol of the risen Christ, and the Easter liturgy and poetry of the Church often refer to Him as the Paschal Lamb and as our Pasch. We shall better understand this usage if we know some relevant points of Jewish history and of Old-Testament ceremonial.

The night before the enslaved Hebrews won the Egyptian ruler's consent to escape to their old homeland, Moses in God's name had ordered them to eat an un-

22

blemished roasted year-old lamb in an austere departure meal. As a holocaust, the lamb was to be eaten entire or all remains of it were to be burnt. Each family was to sprinkle the front doorposts of its dwelling with the lamb's blood.[28]

During that night God and His angels swept over all Egyptian territories, killing the first-born male of every family and of every beast in the land, except those in places which had been sprinkled with lamb's blood. This calamity, which the forewarned Israelites had been spared, finally induced Pharaoh to let the chosen people leave his lands. They started their exodus that night, henceforward to be known as the Passover. For the Lord and His angels passed over the land that night; the Lord's people passed over from slavery to freedom; and they began their passage across the frontiers through the Red Sea. The name, Passing-over or Pasch, was transferred from the event and the night to the meal of lamb eaten that night, much as we use the names Thanksgiving Day, Thanksgiving dinner, and Thanksgiving turkey.

God ordered an annual religious memorial of their deliverance by His power and the blood of the lamb. On a fixed day each year, every Hebrew family was to eat the roasted lamb with herbs and unleavened bread. And a great temple sacrifice of seven perfect lambs was to be offered during the day of the great solemnity. The anniversary was to occupy an octave.[29]

This religious meal was being eaten by our Lord the night before He died. Having finished the Hebrew ritual, He then instituted His own feast of love and His own memorial of the redemption of all peoples in which He, the true Lamb, would be sacrificed and eaten entire, Body and Blood, by the members of His mystical family. On the cross the next day, the divine Lamb died, His body the altar on which His blood was poured while He performed His priestly act of offering His heroic suffering, obedience, and life as a gift to His Father for all men's sins.

Hence, these days of redemption are called the Christian Passover and the paschal season because events and ceremonies in the Jewish Passover had prophetically foreshadowed them. Some of the many parallels may be tabled as follows.

Jewish Passover	Christian Passover
1. Long captivity in Egypt, ruled by a man of alien blood, the Pharaoh	Bondage of all sinners, governed by Satan, helpless to redeem themselves
2. Passover night	The first Holy Thursday; the Easter Vigil
3. Spotless male lamb	Christ, the spotless Son of Mary, the Victim for all men
4. Paschal meal	Holy Communion
5. Saving blood of the lamb	Christ's blood on Calvary protecting and ransoming all men
6. Liberation of Hebrews by angels and Moses	Christ, Redeemer and Liberator of all men
7. Paschal sacrifice	Christ on the Cross and in the Mass
8. Passage through Red Sea	Easter baptisms
9. Pillar of fire leading the people to the Promised Land	Christ leading His Church to heaven. He is symbolized by the Easter candle carried in procession

10. Covenant between God and man on Mt. Sinai	New Testament sealed by Christ's blood on Mt. Calvary
11. New Hebrew (non-pagan) religion, sacrifice, tribal priesthood of Levites	The new Christian religion, Mass, sacramental priesthood
12. Fire of glory from heaven miraculously proves God's acceptance of Aaron's new sacrifice	God glorifies Christ the Victim by the Resurrection and Ascension
13. Moses, the leader; Hebrews, a new independent people	Christ, King and Priest; His people, all the baptized of all nations and races
14. Forty years' march and wandering through the desert	Life on earth a pilgrimage to the promised heaven
15. Annual commemorative services	Easter vigil, day, season; every Mass; every Sunday

Among all the points of comparison, the central idea is the paschal lamb and its functions as food for the journey to the promised land, as object sacrificed, and as protector of the people from God's wrath by its shed blood.

Accordingly, the beautiful line of St. Paul, often used by the Church at Easter, *Christ our Pasch is immolated,*[30] means this. The Lamb is a variant name for Saviour, Redeemer, Jesus. As Head of the redeemed, Christ is the priest who offers to God His human nature, a gift and holocaust for all mankind. He is the victim divinely designated, whose human life exhausts the possibilities of suffering

and is completely consumed in submission to God. By
the shedding of His blood, we are spared from God's anger
and are freed from captivity to sin, from the chains of
fear and superstition, and from the restraints of the Old
Testament. We become a new people gathered from all
nations, Christians, children of God, and followers of
Christ by the grace merited for us by the Lamb. As
children, we eat a divinely supplied food, which is again
the Body and Blood of the Lamb. The Lamb won all
these blessings for all of us, and only the Lamb has redeemed us. God clearly showed His favorable answer to
the Saviour's prayers for mercy because He has clothed the
Victim's dead body with radiant life and has lifted His
human nature to heaven. Christ has *passed over* from
shame to glory, from earth to heaven. At the throne of
God, the Lamb continues to offer Himself for us, whenever holy Mass is repeated in His memory on earth. His
redemption is an immortal success over all the earth and
forever in heaven.

When John the Baptist saw Jesus coming out of the
desert to the River Jordan, he pointed him out to John
and his other disciples in the famous words: "Look, there
is the lamb of God, who takes away the sins of the
world."[31] Echoing these words of his first master, John
the Evangelist often refers to the Saviour as the Lamb
and in the Apocalypse knew Him to be not just a dying
victim, but the living, victorious Lamb on the altar in
heaven.[32] Inspired by St. John's words, our artists picture
Christ sometimes as a live lamb with bloodstained wool,
holding a victory pennant that is decked with a crimson
cross; sometimes as a lamb seated on the great book of
life, which He alone can open; and again as enthroned
at the Father's side in heaven, interceding for us on the
celestial altar and honored by angels and saints. Van

Eyck's *Adoration of the Lamb* is the most majestic of all these artistic honors paid to our paschal Victim.

OUR MEMORIES OF THE LAMB

The Lamb's sufferings, glory, celestial life, and blessings to us deserve our grateful remembrance. Therefore, the Church in our name expresses loving thanks in the annual festivity of Easter and in the preceding days of Holy Week. She replaced the Hebrew seventh day by Sunday as the day set aside for worship, thus better to commemorate Christ's choice of the first day to begin His glory. Indeed, every Mass any day anywhere recalls the Resurrection and Ascension, as well as the Passion and death of Christ.[33] The prayer of the Canon that immediately follows the consecration, the repetition of Christ's words, "Do this in memory of Me," and the elevation assure Christ that we, His servants, obeying His request for a memory, have sacrificed Him anew in memory of His Passion, *Resurrection*, and *Ascension*. Even so, the idea of the Passover Lamb figures more prominently in the Easter services and offices than during the rest of the year. The immolation of the Lamb is mentioned often in the paschal-candle song, in the Gradual of Easter week, in the seasonal Preface, and elsewhere. It is the opening announcement of the Easter play which remains as the Sequence in the Masses of the octave:[34]

> To their paschal Victim
> Christians are offering their praises;
> For the Lamb has redeemed us sheep,
> The spotless Christ has reconciled us sinners to His Father.

The priest holds up Christ to the people before descending to the Communion rail: "Behold the Lamb of God, the Saviour of the world's sins." When we have partaken of the Lamb, we may in thanksgiving acclaim Him with one or other of those salutes which St. John heard filling heaven: "Worthy is the Lamb who has been slain to receive power and wealth and wisdom and strength and honor and glory and blessing."[35] Amen and Alleluia!

We also revive our confidence in the merciful, powerful merits of His precious blood. Since one drop of it shed in love for men was enough to redeem the world,[36] then surely its total outpouring is far more than enough to save my soul, however unworthy and troubled and once hostile it may have been. This hope also leads us to thank God that the Lamb has liberated us from sin and hell. Thanks to our Saviour, who redeemed us at so very great a price.

We praise God for bestowing such glory on the Lamb, His Son, in accepting Him as the heavenly Victim, whose generous blood ever gleams before the sight of God. We praise Him for esteeming this blood, shed so often,[37] as worthy of eternal honor. We thank Him for our Lamb. We look forward to seeing in heaven the same vision that John had: of the wedding of the Lamb with His bride, the Church.

May that loving wedding have its personal copy in my own soul in the perpetual mystical union of Christ with my mind and will.

AGNUS DEI, MERCY AND PEACE![38]

Such a union with Christ is far from achieved in us. While we are marching over the desert of this world toward the Promised Land and promised vision, we need the daily help of the Lamb. We can often make to Him the appealing petition formed by the Church, whose triple

Agnus Dei preceding Communion reminds Christ of some basic blessings which we need every day.

> Lamb of God, You who take away the sins of the world,
>   Show us Your pity.
> Lamb of God, You who take away the sins of the world,
>   Grant us Your mercy.
> Lamb of God, You who take away the sins of the world,
>   Give us Your peace.

Be truly our Saviour and take away our sins. Have mercy on all our needs, especially our need for forgiveness. Give us Your Easter gift to the Apostles: Your peace which the world cannot give and cannot match. May we even ask for the grace to imitate You in sacrificing ourselves and what we have for God's love and the relief of sinners? May we be little lambs united with Your work as the perfect, spotless Lamb of God?[39]

5. THE GRACE OF THE SECOND LIFE

Christ's return to full human life on Easter morning began His second life. It lasted for forty days on earth and will last through endless years in heaven. This second life is an immortal one in both His soul and His body.[40] The Son of Man appearing to St. John said: "I am the First and the Last and the Living One. I was dead, but how wonderful, I live for ever and ever, and have the keys of death and of the nether world."[41] The paschal

Sequence praises the mystery of the death of the King of Life and His victory over death in these lines:

For death and life fought an amazing duel.
The King of Life, though dead a while, now reigns in life.[42]

Adam's sin is responsible for human bodily death and, together with each one's personal serious sins, is responsible for the death of the grace-life in human souls. The one death sunders man's body from his soul; the other sunders man's humanity from his God. The second Adam must crush death in both its forms. It was fitting that the Conqueror of sin should enter into a second life wherein sin, the vanquished, could no more touch Him in any way.

He overcame death by dying for the sake of love; He gave His life for our spiritual lives. He also overcame death by destroying its cause in sin. He overcame it by the triumphant resurgence of His bodily life and the reunion of His immortal soul with His now deathless body.

The Christian copies Christ's victory over death in three similar ways: by despising the terrors of death when the love of God and one's fellows calls one to face death that they may live; by conquering one's sins; and by rising on the last day to new bodily and full human life.

As it is the privileged destiny of the Christian to be conformed to Christ, we are to resemble His second life at two levels and at two moments of our existence.[43] The first level is that of the soul into which Christ's Spirit pours living grace; here and now we have already begun this life of union with God in grace and virtuous action. The second level is in our glorified bodies; its moment begins at the end of the world when our flesh copies His glorious risen body. Both these conformities are the gift of the Redeemer who "by dying has destroyed our death and by rising has restored our life." This truth in the Easter Preface applies to both types of human death and both modes of human resurrection. Our spiritual resurrection occurs in time; our total resurrection takes place in eternity.

Christ claimed to be personally "the Resurrection and the Life,"[44] who gives first life and second life to men because He is Himself the Being and the Cause of life. As God, He is Life itself, undivided, full, unbeginning and unending in His living activity of knowledge and love. Being Life, He originates all life as its creator. He is the cause of the godlike life of grace as well as of all natural life. He is the cause of restoration of life to bodies and to souls. He is the Lord of Life who masters death. As the Son of God and of Mary said of Himself, "I have power to lay down my life and power to take it up again."[45] His resurrection proved His claim. His miracles also proved His claim to heal and restore bodily life and to heal and revive souls buried in sin.

Moreover, Christ in His godhead is our life because the vision of God will be the chief act of our immortal life in heaven. For He is both start and goal of our life for us.

In His human nature, Jesus possesses the fullness of the divine life of grace and wills to impart some of this life to each man. His lifeblood, shed as a gift of life for His brethren, buys for us the divine animation of grace, the vitality of a fervent Christian life, and the restoration of corporeal life on that day when the King of Life summons all the dead to be judged. His merits and rising are the instrumental cause of all human recovery of spiritual grace-life and of bodily risen life. In both these conditions of life, He is the model of life for all men.

BAPTISM, RESURRECTION OF THE SPIRIT

At Easter the Church, though mindful of our distant bodily resurrection, is chiefly concerned with our immediate spiritual resurrection. Led on by the letters of Paul, Peter, and John, the liturgy devotes much attention to converts and the first days of their new lives as Christians risen with Christ from the tomb of the baptismal font. We read many notices of newness in the Church's prayers: the new life, the new man, the new creature, the new people of God, the new law, the new freedom, the new song of Alleluia, the new food, the new paste, the new joy on earth. On the Easter Vigil, devoted to converts, the blessings of the new fire, the new candle, the font, the baptismal water and fresh holy water take place; and baptisms are solemnly administered. The octave is the week of the white-robed; the Sunday after Easter is the Lord's day *in white*; Pentecost, a secondary baptismal feast, is *Whitsunday*.

The adult convert, who joins Christ in baptism, often acutely experiences this change from his old way of life to a new spiritual life in Christ, with new ideas and ideals, new obligations and rights, new ways of praying and loving. It is a far more transforming experience than the start of married or of convent life.

St. Paul has written of the symbolic connection between Christ's resurrection and the convert's rising to the new life of grace in these words to the Colossians:

Buried with him [Christ] by Baptism, you also rose with him by your faith in the power of God who raised him from the dead. At that time when death had come to you from your sins . . . , God brought you to life with Jesus, when he forgave you all your sins. . . .[46]

The Romans heard similar instructions:

> Do you not know that all of us who have been baptized into
> union with Christ Jesus have been baptized into union with his
> death? Yes, we were buried in death with him by means of
> Baptism, in order that, just as Christ was raised from the dead
> by the glorious power of the Father, so we also may conduct
> ourselves by a new principle of life. Now since we have grown
> to be one with him through a death like his, we shall also be
> one with him by a resurrection like his.[47]

The metaphor used here is clear enough. The human
soul, as victim of unforgiven original sin and serious
personal sins, is lacking in grace and is dead and helpless
spiritually. As dead, it wears the grave clothes of the
sinner and is marked for burial. The baptismal font is
the tomb which the sinner who has accepted the new
faith enters. His immersion beneath the baptismal waters
pictures the burial of the old or unforgiven man. After the
consecrating words and waters of baptism have given him
the life of grace, he is lifted from the font, no longer
dead with sin but alive with the Holy Spirit. Emerged
from this tomb, the believer now lives in Christ. Three
stages of the older ceremonial of immersion also indicated
this turning of the sin-deadened soul into a living Christian
soul. The old clothing of the sinner was shucked; the
life-giving waters of the sacrament washed the skin; and
the new white garment of beautiful Christian innocence
symbolized that he had put on Christ and His life as his
own.[48] It would be good if our new gay clothing at Easter
time were a material reminder to us of our baptism and
our need to arise anew with Christ. The shape of some
churches and baptistries resembles tombs or mausoleums in
order to recall Christ's Resurrection and the secret resurrec-
tions of souls which in these places rise from sin.

For centuries the Easter Vigil was the preferred time

for admitting grown men and women into the life of
Christ within His Church. The surrender to Christ made
by the new converts seemed to be a special sign of Christ's
continuing victory over sin and sorrow. Their conversion
and gifts of grace were a special source of Easter joy for
the whole Christian family. Their rising with Christ
prompted a renewal of faith and love in "old" Christians,
who would welcome, sponsor, help, pray for, and be inspired by the fervor of their new brethren.

Though Easter baptisms are nowadays few, all attending the vigil service proclaim their faith in the risen Christ
by reciting the Creed, and they dedicate themselves anew
to a holy Christian life by renewing their baptismal promises and receiving the blessing of the new paschal water.
The use of holy water in and out of Church also can
revive the spirit of our baptismal rising with Christ.
A decorated baptistry is one of the special features of
Easter, ranking next to the paschal candle in the sanctuary
as the Easter analogue of the crib of Christmas.

LEADING THE RISEN LIFE

As Christ is the model of Christian living, His forty
days of glorious life on earth are meant for our fervent
imitation. Once He has entered our lives, we can never
be the same old sinners. Once dead to sin and self, we
are expected to stay permanently rid of sin and to keep
the disordered self permanently under the mastery of
the spirit. St. Paul speaks to Colossians and Romans[49] of
this life of those who are risen with Christ. They are to
set their minds on things above which quicken the Christ-
life, not on earthly things which crush it. They are to
put to death such earthly things as their passions, acts
of lust, evil desires, deeds of avarice, angry outbursts, foul

language, and lies. They are to strip off the old self with
its typical deeds and put on the new Christlike self, thus
clothing themselves with compassion, kindness, humility,
and gentleness. Loving one another, they are to bear with
one another and forgive as Christ has forgiven them. If
they love one another and become truly one body in
Christ, the peace of Christ will rule in their hearts, the
joy of Christ will rise in their spiritual songs, and the glory
of God will be proclaimed through their thanks. Those
buried with Christ in baptism and risen with Him must
crucify the old self and keep it dead to sin, for spiritual
death does not befit one who follows the immortal Christ.
They are to consecrate themselves and their members to
God and a holy life. Men freed from the dominion of sin,
they are to bear Christ's lively grace.

This outline of the virtues of the soul risen with Christ
presents both a personal and a community obligation. For
Christ is to live in me personally and in His whole body.
I must let Christ enter or re-enter my life, and I must
shape my new life according to the risen Christ in my
beliefs, principles, graces, and deeds. But I must also
rejoice at Easter in the blessings of all other Christians
and I must pray for and contribute to the life of the
complete Christ contained in His many members. For
we have been spiritually raised up together. Together we
form a new kingdom, a chosen race, a holy people, a
royal priesthood[50] who march in love to the Promised
Land.

If Christ deeply lives in me, I shall learn to see His
living beauty in all those who have been raised to a second
life by faith, baptism, and forgiveness in Christ Jesus.

6. THE GRACE OF FORGIVENESS

As Christ rises at Easter, so must all the members of His Church rise. His members will rise in body only on the last day. The ungraced rise in spirit for the first time on the day of their baptism. The baptized who have fallen from grace rise in spirit for a second and a thousandth time when their mortal sins are pardoned in the sacrament of penance.

The condition of the defeated soul of Adam was painted

by God in the defeat of his body by death. For death, in destroying life, despoils the body of energy and beauty and leaves it helpless, passive, and decaying. This same powerlessness and rottenness infects the soul of a serious sinner. For the time being, he is supernaturally dead. It was nobly fitting that the new life-giving Adam should restore spiritual life, not once only but countless times, by giving his priests the power to raise spiritually dead members of the Church to new spiritual life. It was specially suitable that the Saviour should choose Easter Day for founding this sweet sacrament of pardon for the penitent. In this way the Lord of Life celebrates His victory over sin by setting up a permanent court with power to heal sinners; and the victory of Easter will go on and on in many millions of absolutions of the guilty.

The moment and the situation chosen by Christ for this paschal gift are most interesting. The exciting news that He is alive again has been circulating all day. The women have seen the open tomb, the grave clothes, and the angels. They and Magdalene have looked on the glorified Lord. Peter and John have verified the facts that the grave is empty and that the shroud has been carefully folded. Peter has made his peace in a meeting with his Master. It is evening.[52] The Apostles and other friends are dining together, rehearsing the evidence, trying to accustom their imaginations and feelings to this surprising turn of events. While they debate the probabilities, Cleophas and his companion breathlessly tell of their walk and dinner with the risen Lord. The debate grows warmer. Those who have seen Him can be shaken by no objection. Believers argue with the skeptics, the convinced with the hopeful. If this is fact not mere rumor, what should they do next? Go to Galilee, as the message of the women directed? If He were alive, they might see Him there. The unbelieving would yield to that test of the personal presence of Christ. In any case they will be safer away from Jerusalem if Christ's baffled enemies begin reprisals.

Then to settle their problem, without knocking or unbolting the door, without any sound of movement, the glorious Saviour enters, takes a place among them, and speaks in His well-known voice: "Peace be to you!"[53]

They need this perfect greeting. The suddenness of His coming, His disregard of limiting spatial conditions, His very splendor shocks them. He lets them gaze at Him and become a little used to Him. He can hear their pounding hearts. He calms and encourages them. He lets their senses surely grasp His reality. One with hands and feet and with a mouth that speaks and eats broiled fish before their eyes is a true body, not a ghost or image in a dream.

After their tense critical sight has yielded to His persuasive being, He shows them deeper levels of meaning in His wish for their peace. His friendly way tells them that He knows of their grief over His Passion and of their distress over their own failure to stand boldly by Him. Their adoration and belief serve for contrition; His acceptance is His pardoning. He gives them another form of peace, peace of mind, by explaining to them how necessary it was that the Messias should suffer, die, and rise again. But more, He will make them ministers of His peace to men, peacemakers to carry the gifts of the Resurrection to men at the ends of the world and to the end of time.

This surely is one of history's greatest moments when the Prince of Peace sets up His Easter memorial in this new sacrament of peacemaking. He now fulfills a promise given a year or so ago that He would empower them to bind and loose all things on earth and that their decision here would be ratified in heaven above. He confers this promised power on them. He makes it clear that it reaches even to the remission or retention of sins, though these be offenses against God Himself. This is God's own Son, the Redeemer of all sins, the Liberator from all captivity to Satan, the Judge of all souls, who hands on this divine power to the priests of His Church for the needy in spirit among His members.

MERCIFUL JUDGES

Jesus then said again to the delighted disciples: "Peace be to you! As the Father has made me his ambassador, so I am making you my ambassadors."

Then He breathed on them and said: "Receive the Holy Spirit. Whenever you remit anyone's sins, they are remitted; when you retain anyone's sins, they are retained."[54]

"In the name of the Messias, the need of a change of heart and forgiveness of sins must be preached to all nations."[55]

It is all a message of peace. Ever consistent with His own character and mission, the Prince of Peace who had come at Christmas today passes on to them His mission of redeeming sinners. For He was an ambassador not only of divine truth but of divine mercy, too. As sinners are ever with us, this power of forgiving is a permanent endowment of Christ's Church.

The gift is imparted with an increase of the divine Spirit of Holiness, of Love, of Mercy, and of Judgment. It must be the Spirit of God who forgives, in union with the Father and Son, who have sent Him to forgive and to consecrate human ministers of divine pardon. It must be the Spirit of Holiness who banishes wickedness and restores the holy life of sanctifying grace to sinful souls. And so the absolving priest rightly says to one who has confessed: "I release you from your sins in the name of the

Father and of the Son and of the Holy Spirit." The Blessed
Trinity forgives, and the sins remain forever forgiven.

It may be harder to understand that the Holy Spirit
is given to our priests as the Spirit of Judgment. Our
Lord at the Last Supper explained to the Apostles that
the promised Spirit was the judge of innocence and guilt.[56]
Authoritative judging of the deeds and misdeeds of souls
is a divine work, and forgiveness is a divine work. The
Holy Spirit of Judgment makes the Apostles judges of
guilt, who can free from sin and restore to grace or decide
officially who are unworthy of pardon because they lack
sincerity and change of heart. What the Apostles forgive,
the Holy Spirit forgives. In removing mortal guilt, the
Spirit recreates sanctifying grace in the human soul and
Himself returns to inhabit that soul. For either mortal
guilt or sanctifying grace are in the soul of one baptized;
they are never present together; the one shuts out the
other.

As judges delegated by God, priests must act according
to the laws of the kingdom of Christ. And of course, one
of the laws of this supreme King and Judge is that there
is no forgiveness without repentant contrition and resolu-
tion. But even this grace of genuine contrition is a gift
of the Saviour to the soul, preparing it for the act of
confessing and the reception of liberation from guilt.

Through his priests, therefore, Christ's Easter gift of
forgiveness persists through many centuries. Like Him,
they judge His friends and foes, penitent and impenitent.
They are His agents of mercy and of justice, comforters
of the contrite guilty and punishers of those who resist
His merciful love. When the priest absolves, the angels
of the Resurrection rejoice over the sinner who does
penance. In the confessional Christ extends His generous
act of forgiving the thief on the cross to whosoever

asks to be readmitted to His kingdom. For with forgiveness we regain all our rights to live with Christ in time and in eternity.

Christ's choice of the festive day of victory, Easter, for this sacrament's founding reveals His own sweet attitude to this sacrament and to all who approach it. This is indeed the Peacemaker's act of reconciling the estranged and reuniting the members with their Head. This is a victorious King's big-souled amnesty to deserters and rebels. The blood of Christ, the price of our peace, bought the blessings of this sacrament for us.

The priest often dismisses the forgiven penitent with the gracious wish: "Go in peace." Go, forgiven friend of Christ, filled with Christ's paschal peace. Confession and absolution will remain forever bathed in the glory of Christ's resurrection once we understand all this. Artists with insight do not build confessionals which are somber prison cells; they decorate them in festive blues and golds and with images of the risen Friend and the Dove of Peace.

THE RISEN SPIRIT

St. Paul's comment about new converts applies well to those reconverted from their sins: God, rich in mercy, was moved by the intense love with which He loved us, and when we were dead by reason of our evildoing, He made us live with the life of Christ.[57]

The genius of the Holy Spirit residing in the Church directed her to command serious sinners to do penance during Lent, to repent, and to receive sacramental absolution during the Easter season. This duty is to be attended to at this season since the grace of this sacrament is a spiritual image of Christ's resurrection. The fallen soul rises up. The life of Christ again blooms in it. A greater wonder than rising from bodily death occurs when He restores the life of grace to the ungraced helpless soul. When the freshly absolved sinner walks forth from the confessional, He is the spiritual copy of Christ walking forth from His tomb to a better life. Such is the tender stooping of His mercy to us; such, His divine initiative in reviving our souls.

This splendid coming-to-life of pardoned men is an immense source of Easter joy not only for Christ and for the forgiven, but for all of us who rejoice with Christ. So many millions have had the Holy Spirit breathe on them again in this sacrament and restore life to their withered souls. Strange and wonderful victory: peace and pardon for all who wish for it.

It behooves us when we are risen again with Christ, never, never again to fall away from Him, but to remain loyal, as the pardoned Apostles did. It behooves us who were so sick in soul frequently to take the tonic of the Eucharistic food to help us return to perfect spiritual health. It behooves us to live as worthy witnesses of the gift of life by remaining dead to self but vitally active in Christ. It is right that as Christ has forgiven us, we forgive others.[58] Thus we will increase His paschal peace among men.

7. THE GRACE OF HEAVENLY DESIRES

The Christian puts to himself one searching question at Easter: Am I risen with Christ? One proof that one is living the risen life of grace is a heart burning with love of Christ and all that belongs to this Friend of our souls. For this must be a feature of the new life of grace that we have a buoyant interest in Christ and a keen ambition to possess His treasures.

If we listen to the Church urging us to live the Christ-life more fully these days, we will spiritually rise from our religious sloth, our moral faults, and our absorption in worldly interests that take the mind and heart away from the risen Lord. It would be a pitiable mistake to let the slackening of the Lenten penances become at Easter a signal for a decrease in our daily living for and yearning for Christ. The paschal season ought rather be a sustained climactic union of our souls with His joy and victories.

The angels standing by the slab of the opened tomb have a message for all of us. They said: You have nothing to fear. We know that you are looking for Jesus of Nazareth who was crucified. But He is risen; He is not here. See the place where He lay. He goes before you to Galilee, as He predicted. There you shall see Him.[59] The angelic welcome is based on their search for Jesus. This sincere motive, interest in Jesus and service to Him rather than selfish curiosity, is what they would recommend to all of us. Seek for Jesus; all will be well. You will find Him, risen of course, whether in Galilee or elsewhere. And having Him, you will have all that can bring you joy. But do not seek Him in the tomb. Do not seek Him in the graveyard of your sins. Do not seek Him in the buried past. Seek the true, living Jesus. "Seek and you shall find."[60]

One of the major instructions of the Church to her children at the Easter season is that they put their minds on heavenly things and look to heaven as the Apostles did at His final departure. Their upturned faces should be copied by our minds ascending heavenward to our beloved Lord. This is one more way of living the risen life.

Desires for spiritual goods, as well as these goods themselves, are gifts of God. Thoughts of heavenly goods and cravings for them are actual graces coming from the Holy Spirit. But we can do our part in preparing for these graces, accepting them, fostering them, and deepening

them. The Church tells us how to do so. First, she sets
the stage for the Spirit's action within us by bringing
back the annual memory of Christ's glorified body and His
entrance into heaven. These remembered truths awaken
us earth-bound men to a better appreciation of invisible
spiritual benedictions which God would gladly bestow
upon us. Appreciation stirs hunger in the soul. This hunger
is fed by the promises of Christ to shower these heavenly
benefits on us if we faithfully follow Him.

Recognizing that such desires are a heavenly gift beyond
our unhelped reach, the Church in her paschal prayers
often animates us to pray for these. She opens the Easter
Vigil by blessing the new fire, begging God that through
this feast of Easter we may be inflamed with heavenly
desires and come with pure minds to the festival of
Christ's undying radiance.[61] After the first prophecy we
pray so to lead our new life that we may persevere in
combating sinful desires and may win everlasting joys.
Other liturgical prayers of the season direct us to love what
God commands, desire what He promises, and keep our
hearts fixed on true joys amid life's changing patterns.
We are urged to pray for thoughts and desires of the right.
On Ascension day we join in requesting that our minds
may dwell in heaven where our Redeemer now is living.[62]
On the Vigil of Pentecost we ask the Holy Spirit for
burning heavenly desires and deep draughts of life.[63] Perhaps the most remarkable of these petitions for a heaven-
bent mind occurs on the fifth Sunday after Pentecost:

> O God, who have prepared invisible goods
>   for those who love You:
>   pour into our hearts a longing for Your love,
>   so that by loving You in all things and more than all things,
>   we may attain Your promises
>   which outrun every desire and expectation.
>   Through Christ our Lord.

The Postcommunion of the Mass of the Sacred Heart, charged with the spirit of charity, begs for a love of heavenly things and contempt for earthly ones. Indeed, so great is the wish of the Church that we often lift our attention heavenward that she joyously bids us at each day's Preface: *Sursum corda*, Lift up your hearts.

If only our daily answer were completely true: We have them lifted up to the Lord.

Set Your Mind on Things Above[64]

The numerous gifts which we desire from our heavenly Father include knowledge of God in His wonderful Trinity; the love of God and of His Son, Jesus Christ; longing for God's glory; craving for the company of Christ; willing of the will of God in our lives and its accomplishment in the conduct of others; sanctifying grace and its growth; opportunities to practice many Christian virtues; union with Christ laboring and suffering for our redemption; universal justice and the reign of Christ's peace on earth; heaven, the sight of Jesus, our rewards, and the means to get to heaven; contentment with our Father's provident care over us; and all other gifts for which the Spirit working in our souls urges us to plead.[65]

The swinging of the mind towards higher things and its flight from the lower may be a critical moment in the development of the interior Christian life. As the divine captures our attention and deepens our motives, we begin to get rid of our preferences for bodily comforts, worldly honors, and temporal blessings. These things lose their former importance in our estimation. Earth, after all, is but for a while; heaven is forever. The means, the goods of time, are far below the end — God — in value. A true rating of the worth of earthly things is sometimes

spoken of as contempt for them. Though we need not regard them as wicked or worthless, yet part of the spiritual
effort to live with Christ risen must consist in counteract-
ing all those desires that shut spiritual goods out of our
lives. Those things which the world hostile to Christ, our
own unreasonable flesh, and the tempting devil would give
us if we but wanted them, must be banished from our
choices. We must not let ourselves be overthrown by
worldly desires, as was the rich young man who approached
our Lord. Love of the pleasures of sense is the cockle that
chokes the good seed of Christ's truth in the lives of
average sinners. Love of honors in this world pulls other
stronger souls away from Christ.

All such desires that stand against Christ's mastery
within us must be controlled, starved, and never allowed
to compete with our desires for the gifts of Christ. To
win this freedom from choosing these earthly, selfish, and
evil things usually takes long spiritual training. That is
why the ascetic life must mark those who are risen with
Christ. A religious vocation by demanding daily sacrifices
greatly assists this denial of self; and this death of the self
leads to detached purity of heart with regard to lower
goods. But in or out of the religious state, every Christian
who would be close to Christ must labor for his spiritual
freedom from all things except God and His will.[66]

Besides her suggestions on prayer and combating worldly
desires, the Church also tells us to think. "Set your minds
on things above," she repeats from St. Paul when he was
advising Christians risen from sin. Turn the mind to the
divine and the good; let these heavenly blessings seize your
imaginations, thoughts, and affections. Cardinal Newman
echoed St. Paul in this bit of advice: "Let me put my
mind on things above, and in God's good time He will set
my heart on things above." Desire follows knowledge.

One of the ways to holiness is to long for it. One of the paths to heaven is to desire heaven. If I but occupy my mind with God, it will not be long before He will shower on me an interest in and love for these heavenly goods. Love will soar heavenward where our thoughts have already risen.

The Church further suggests that we cultivate holy desires by giving some of our time to spiritual reading. From it we can gain higher esteem for spiritual realities, a sense of true values, a closer mental affinity with the judgment of Christ, and a centering of thoughts and sentiments on the treasures of the soul. The Church, moreover, admiringly points out to us saints whose lives seemed to be a flame of desire for heaven and a leap of the spirit toward Christ. St. Paul desired to be dissolved in order to be with Christ. The autobiographies of the two saints Teresa and the letters of St. Margaret Mary are famous examples of souls absorbed in thoughts of heaven. The practical St. Ignatius Loyola sighed deeply when he looked at the silvery stars and felt how petty was earth when he turned his thoughts to heaven beyond the stars. St. Stanislaus Kostka, dead at eighteen, had three great irrepressible longings which summed up his whole spiritual life: the desire for Holy Communion, the desire for the religious life, and the desire for heaven.[67] Many a martyr fixed his mind on heaven while his body suffered.

JOURNEYING TO THE PROMISED LAND

When the wings of the spirit spring upward, we will take the right means to make heavenly goods come true in our lives. Our conduct will become more heavenly in quality. Desire will become hope, and hope will carry us forward to our meeting with Jesus in heaven.

During these years on earth we are fugitives and pilgrims journeying to the Promised Land where our Father dwells and which we are to inherit. In our Passover years while we slowly travel from the land of slavery to sin through the barren Sinai desert of this world, we must not give way to foolish longings for Egypt's fleshpots, to the weariness of the long march, and to disappointment with our long waiting before we come into the promised kingdom. With high hope we must keep reaching forward to the wonders which God is preparing for us in our final homeland. That is one reason why Easter is so spiritually helpful in giving us glimpses of His glory and strengthening our hopes to possess it. God knows how to slake our thirst for Himself, and He means to give Himself, face-to-face and heart-to-heart, to all who rise with His Son. "When Christ, your life, appears, then you shall appear with him in glory."[68]

Each Sunday, we are taught, is a little Easter, a weekly memorial of our Saviour's resurrection. Let me, then, at least on Sunday, put earth aside and climb closer to God by the ladder of heavenly desires.

Father in heaven, bring me to heaven. Father of Christ, bring me to Christ.

8. THE GRACE OF THE VICTOR'S CROWN

THE RISEN SOLDIER

Victory is another plain meaning of Christ's escape from His sepulcher. His second life, regarded as testimony to His divine success, deeply impressed the Apostles, whose recorded preaching is filled with it. Peter, Paul, and the others saw that the Resurrection climaxes the life, miracles, and teachings of Christ and that it dramatically explains the whole plan of man's salvation by the cross. For salvation pertains to the genuine success of souls; and the rightness of Christ's saving design boldly appears in His bodily triumph which, in turn, manifests the triumph of His spirit and His truths.

We may measure the greatness of the Lord's victory by the seeming completeness of His defeat on Calvary, by the strength of the forces which He vanquished, by the splendid prizes which He won, and by the perpetuity of His conquests.

When the fallen Leader bowed His bruised head and expired, He looked utterly broken. The Lord of Glory had indeed let Himself be emptied of His majesty and had been degraded to the class of crime-laden slaves. Besides the personal tragic loss of His life and honor, His followers were routed, His reputation among the people had been blackened, and His kingdom had gone down in ruins. The thorny brow pictured for every one how inglorious a king He was. Almost the whole world seemed to be against Him.

If he were to win now, what forces must He defeat? Nature's full strength would keep His body dead. Israel's leaders, Rome's officials and legionaries, and Satan's mischief-making with human weaknesses would stay combined against Him. Men's fear, pride, love of pleasure, and disbelief; humiliating memories of His crucifixion, shame at having followed a dead condemned leader, terror of sharing in His unjust treatment, and despair of a lost cause: all these must be overcome if He is to win human loyalties now. Is such a victory probable or even possible? Who ever wins a battle with death? What soldier comes back, when slain, to face His enemies again, to regroup His forces, to win greater contests after his death? Only God is mighty enough to face such enemies and such obstacles and win in the end.

But Christ *is* God. He had foreseen His seeming defeat.

He had predicted His victory after His death and because
of His death.

Several gleams of success relieved His dying hours. One
thief had turned to Him as King of the world-to-come.
The centurion honored Him as different from all other
men. The veil of the Temple, stronghold of the enemy,
was ripped by nature. Nicodemus and Joseph of Arimathea broke with the Sanhedrin in order to give noble
burial to the King of Martyrs. Trembling Pharisees, fear-
ing Him in death, sued for a guard to keep Him dead.
For they recalled His confident challenge that He would
rebuild His holy body within three days after they should
have destroyed Him. If only they could prove that absurd
speech of defiance to be false; then, after three days, He
would drop into eternal oblivion, and they would remain
masters of the field.

Strange victory wrought out of the very materials of
His defeat! A martyr's triumph by innocence and penance,
prayer and forgiveness, patience and obedience! Francis
Thompson expresses our surprise at this way of winning
in *The Veteran of Heaven:*

> What is this, unheard before,
> that the Unarmed makes war,
> And the Slain hath the gain,
> and the Victor hath the rout?
> What wars, then, are these,
> and what the enemies,
> Strange Chief, with the scars
> of Thy conquest trenched about?[69]

What has He won for Himself and for us? For conquests and prospects show the value of the victory.

He won all that He stood for, prayed for, and suffered
for. The Lord of Life defeated death together with its
causes in sin and with its effects in mourning, decay, fear,
and the pointless ending of man in a grave. The Victor

exultantly proclaims Himself the Resurrection and the Life, not the victim of doom and death. St. Paul boasts of Christ's victory over all His enemies, even over the last enemy, death, and mocks at it: Death is swallowed up in victory. O death, where is thy former victory? What has happened to that biting sting of thine?[70]

It is a victory for justice. First, God's justice has been satisfied by the enormous price of the agonies and blood-sheddings of His Son offered in vicarious penance for the guilty. And God's court of justice has raised Him to life to prove that human courts of justice sentenced Him wrongly. The right side has won.

It is a victory for freedom. Christ has liberated His people from the chains of guilt, barred the doors of hell against man's easy entrance into it, restored innocence and the liberty of children to Christian hearts, checked the raging careers of hate, cruelty, irreverence, and injustice, introduced the paschal peace between God and man, and inaugurated the kingdom of the freed in His Church on earth.

Divine power has conquered the archenemy, Satan, and all the cohorts of this Prince of the World. The Lamb has slain the beast and all the kings who were allied with him.[71] The Christian smiles to think how Lucifer, his might broken, bends his knee at the sound of the holy name and runs like a rabbit from a drop of holy water. All Christ's enemies are red-faced and bewildered at their powerlessness to do any lasting harm. Lucifer's own tool, death to Christ, has become a trap to undo the grip of evil over unhappy men.

In the Resurrection, mercy marched to victory over the guilty who seek His pardon. The repentant witness Him tearing up the handwriting of the decree against them.

This is God's victory for the sake of truth. All doubts

on Christ's claims to be God and the leader of men now look foolish. Skepticism, ignorance, error, and false cults are stamped out. False gods and false philosophers are unmasked by His light. Human values are transformed since men now can know the importance of God, of Christ, and of their own souls.

Due honor is victorious over dishonor. Because Christ obediently humbled Himself to very death, God has given Him a name above every name, that precious name, Jesus, before which every knee in heaven, on earth, and below earth bends down.[72] Because of His life of obedient service, His Father has made Him the king of the living and their judge.

It is a victory of love, attesting the love of the Father for His only-begotten Son and confirming all the gifts which Christ's love has heaped upon us.

Moreover, Christ the Unconquered has divinely assured prospects that His victory will last. His Church is infallible and will endure throughout time. His name is imperishable, and no other name can ever approach its high glory. The mounting centuries and human conquests can only add to His honors. Heaven is His. After the Last Judgment will have given universal evidence of His glory, He will be but beginning His eternal rule over all the redeemed in the City of God and over the new heaven and the new earth. His Father has gladly heard His prayer and given Him the glory which He had before the world was.[73]

CONQUER IN THIS SIGN!

A conqueror's joy has a delight of its own, other than the joy of the mind's discoveries and other than the joy of knowing oneself beloved and blessed by another. Conflict, courage, sacrifice, decision, blood, sweat, tears, anguish, one's own efforts accomplish good deeds for God under His holy commands, and they deserve a reward from God. Though God's grace empowers the victor and His generosity gives the rewards, yet the fighter has earned the spoils as his own right because he has authored the results by his free decision, his responsible planning, his persevering patience, and his costly sacrifices. The glory shining on Christ at Easter is brighter than that of the heavens at His birth and of His own body at His transfiguration. His five wounds declare His own free part in His amazing and total victory.

It is proper that we imagine this King and Victor as wearing a crown on Easter day. The crown is an ancient symbol of royalty, of military success, and of championship in any competition. The crown of thorns on the suffering Soldier has become a jeweled halo that speaks of His many-sided victory. We should crown Him with many crowns: of kingship, of truth, of beauty, of love, of power, and of peace. We might even wear our academic and civic regalia, our robes of office, and our Easter finery as decorations honoring His Easter crown.

The cross itself and the crucifix have become signs of triumphant charity. Christ's enemies made the cross the symbol which displayed their utter contempt of Him. He took it up as His standard of loving conquest. "I, once I have been lifted up from the earth, will draw all men to Myself."[74] As suited a triumphant object, the crucifix in earlier centuries was made of precious woods and other valuable materials, was adorned with precious stones, gold, and enamels, and presented the Saviour wearing royal garments and a golden crown. As crucifixes in this style were common in churches, the custom of veiling them during Passiontide arose since their glorious appearance did not well consort with the theme of the suffering, disrobed Redeemer. The unveiling of these glorified crucifixes on Good Friday splendidly revealed the victory of the cross. In contrast, the act of unveiling the cross in modern Western churches tends rather to reveal the poignancy of the bodily passion of Christ.

As honor to the cross always honors the victorious Christ, we use it at the head of all our processions, for we are marching behind Christ toward heaven. Our rubrics wisely order the use of the sign of the cross in blessing persons and objects in order that His conquests, shared with us, may fend off evils and dispense to us the rewards which He has merited. The faithful, too, understand this way of honoring their Saviour. Though someone not loving Christ might easily feel disgust if invited to kiss the wounds of the Crucified, lovers of Christ take pleasure in adoring and comforting Him by their kisses placed on His image.

Some of our greatest hymns also hail the cross: the *Exultet* or paschal-candle song and the two hymns of Venantius, *Vexilla Regis Prodeunt* ("The King's Banners Are Flying") and *Pange, lingua, gloriosi*:

> Sing, my tongue, the glorious battle . . .
> Sound the high triumphant lay . . .
> How the Victim won the day.[75]

How many millions of times have these acclamations filled choirs, churches, and crusaders' tents.

The famous vision of Constantine when marching to Rome illustrates the power of the cross. The day before the decisive Battle of the Milvian Bridge, he saw in the sky a cross and the legend, "In this sign you shall conquer." He ordered his legions to carry battle-standards with this sign instead of their usual superstitious trimmings. Constantine's victory ended the persecution of the

Church and led to his official favors. Whatever be the detailed historical facts of his vision, Christian judgment was altogether right in attributing the new peace of the Church to the glorious help of the crucified and risen King.

We may regard the message given to Constantine as addressed to us today. "In this sign you shall conquer." Those who labor and suffer under the cross always win. Those who carry their small crosses with Christ, as new Cyrenes who help and are helped by the Saviour, shall enter into glory alongside Christ. "If we endure, we shall also reign with Him."[76]

CHRIST CROWNS HIS OWN

The Church, the Kingdom of the Cross, is one magnificent outcome of His victory. Our victories over self, the world, and the powers of evil are His spiritual successes in us. We have inherited His merits. Through His blood we receive grace, correspond with grace, and hold grace until death. He, the King of Grace, sets crowns of immortality upon all the redeemed when they enter the kingdom prepared by His Father. That we shall be crowned for bearing our trials is His promise. "Be faithful until death, and I will give you the crown which belongs to life."[77] His success in winning the crown foretells our success. Our concern is not the surety of His intentions to reward us, but our own fulfillment of the conditions attached to the promise; and these are that we take up our assigned cross, deny our foolish feelings and self-will, and allow Christ to triumph in our desires, motives, and deeds.

The splendor and the joy of each one's crown is in proportion to the deserts of each. Christ's better friends, His generous martyrs, patient cross-bearers, innocent penitential victims for others, and daring heroes will have fairer crowns and happier days than the less gifted. On that final coronation day when Christ presents the crowned heads of all the redeemed to His heavenly Father and offers His kingdom of justice and truth, of grace and love to the glory of God, the victory of Christ will be complete.

St. Michael, angel of victory, defend me until that day.

May Christ conquer me and all in me that opposes His will. May His courage shine in me in the day of battle for His cause. May His mercy let me share His cross. May His triumph put an unfading crown on one more of His risen soldiers.

9. THE GRACE OF FAITH

The blessing which our Saviour pronounced on believers in the familiar episode with the apostle Thomas is referred to as a ninth beatitude, added to the eight promises contained in the Sermon on the Mount. During the first week of Easter, Thomas did not show himself a model of prompt belief although his stubbornness makes him an excellent witness. His reluctance to accept the Resurrection contrasts sharply with Peter's readiness to believe in

Christ's divine sonship at Caesarea.[78] He lagged far behind John whose observations of the careful folding of the grave clothes brought him to believe even before he had seen the Lord.[79]

Thomas, for reasons not given, was absent on Easter night when the risen Lord visited the Apostles.[80] When these had told the facts to him, he held out against their unanimous eyewitness. "Unless I see in his hands the print of the nails and put my finger into the place where the nails were, I am not going to believe." His doubting insistence on seeing and touching for himself scarcely complimented the word of the others. Yet Thomas was intensely interested in the report. He wished it were true. Fear did not delay his credence, for he was the brave man who had said less than two weeks before, "Let us go along and die with him," as He went to Lazarus' grave.[81]

We must guess at his reasons for doubting. Was it a difficulty for his mind or his will? Perhaps his was a cautious temperament in the face of the new and unusual. Or after the searing disappointment of the Passion, he may have been afraid of being duped by any enthusiasm. Perhaps the totally unexpected character of the event, its puzzling mysteries, its natural impossibility made him refuse to accept the testimony of others. Deep shock over the Master's death may have put him into a hopeless mood. At least, he had not deserted the band of Apostles, though some break seemed to threaten because of his unbelief. He could not reply to their evidence or explain the empty tomb. He resisted their reminders of the Master's predictions of His resurrection and of His several miracles of raising other dead persons. After a week he was still keeping up His fight against grace. Then Jesus condescended to meet Thomas' considerable terms of surrender in a second general visit to the Apostles.

He entered the same room as last week with the same
suddenness and the same opening greeting: "Peace be to
you!" Then the gloriously shining Saviour addressed
Thomas:

> Let me have your finger; put it here, and look at my hands.
> Now let me have your hand, and lay it into my side.
> And do not go on being a doubter: become a believer.[82]

He had not let Mary Magdalene touch Him; He ordered
Thomas to do so and went beyond Thomas' wish to touch
the nail prints by making him put his hand into His
heart. Having complied with the order, Thomas burst into
his wondering adoration: "My Lord and my God!" At
that Jesus said:

> Is it because you have seen me that you have come to believe?
> Happy those who, though they did not see, yet become believers.

In one moment Jesus did several remarkable things. He
accepted Thomas' contrite apology and his adoring faith
in His divinity. He defended the right of the Apostles to
be believed when they give their witness about Him. He
expressed His disappointment in Thomas who wanted
vision before faith, who had not taken the word of his
brethren, and who had failed in hope. He explained for
all times the difference between seeing and believing.
And He uttered His paschal blessing on those who believe without the special privilege of seeing Him risen
with His wounds and who are content to rely on the
word of His accredited ambassadors.

Because he saw and touched the risen body, Thomas
accepted as true that Jesus was risen. But this is not faith
in the Resurrection; this is immediate evidence compelling the senses and the reason. Upon acceptance of the
fact, Thomas under the motion of grace saw its implica-
tion as proving the divinity of Christ and as validating

all His previous teachings. At once he makes amends by a prompt and full act of belief in these other truths, for his natural powers of knowing had no personal evidence of these mysteries.

THREE QUESTIONS ABOUT BELIEF

The blessing to believers which closes the incident deserves loving reflection on three questions. What is this good of faith whose possession should make believers happy? Why do believers deserve a reward? What reward will be given them?

The first question is answered by this fact that the assent of faith is a multiple gift of God and a start toward countless future blessings from heaven.

Faith is a sheer, unearned gift of God to the human soul.[83] It is the first step in God's supernatural romance with the soul; the beginning, root, and foundation of one's salvation. It is God's call to know Him better and through knowledge to come to contrition, hope, baptism, love, and, finally, to eternal union with God.

It is a gift of knowledge or wisdom to the mind; for God interiorly moves the intellect to accept His revealed truths, which are profound and most important. It is a gift of loving obedience to the will, for it kindles the human desire to make the truth one's own and to honor God's kindness in making Himself and His will known to us. This set of graces within the soul may be accompanied by external helps and signs which suggest to us the believability of the doctrines or arouse our interest in them or overcome fears, prejudices, and misunderstandings.

Following the act of faith and the reception of baptism, the sacrament of faith, comes the added gift of the virtue or habit of faith. This is permanently present and active in the Christian soul unless a serious sin against faith voluntarily destroys this habit.

By faith the human intellect shares God's truth. Hence, faith is spoken of as a light. It is sent into our minds by Christ, the Light of the World, and the Holy Spirit, "the Light of Hearts." Being light, it removes from our minds dark ignorance about divine truths. Sometimes it also banishes errors on religion and morals. It frees us from many dangers and opens to the will the road to right spiritual progress. St. Paul's physical blindness, helpless groping, and solitary misery before He accepted Christ's divine sonship and resurrection depict his voluntary spiritual blindness to the truths of faith during his days as a persecutor.[84] But faith brought inner light and healed his physical blindness.

To joyous appreciation of faith as a mark of God's personal love is joined the calm of mind after struggle and the quiet of conscience in obeying the will of God. The new believer in Christ also begins to share a new religious social life with other believers, who are united with him in believing the same doctrines and in worshiping through the sacraments and sacrifice of the Mass. One is guided for the future by infallible religious teaching authority and, if he so wishes, may enjoy the benefits of Catholic educational activity.

Moreover, we know that the Author of our faith prayed for us believers the night of His entrance into His agony[85] and that He died to win the first and the persevering graces of faith for us. Faith, therefore, shows God's generosity to us.

Our second question asks why a gift from God like this deserves a reward to us.

The reward for the assent of faith comes because man's free will welcomes the divine favor. God does not force faith on us; and the truths proposed lie beyond the reach of our intellect's own resources, for we can see them neither by senses nor by reason in any premises. Good will freely acting must direct the intellect to say: "Yes, that's so; I am willing to believe. I do believe." Hence, the act of believing God revealing is both a free gift of God to us and a free gift of our will and mind's co-operation with God. Since the believer chooses to believe, his act is a service to God, worthy of some reward. Faith makes a very agreeable Easter gift to our Lord. He upbraided the Apostles and Thomas for giving it grudgingly.

What the believing mind has before it are the authority of God revealing some truths, and some supporting indications from miracles and prophecies that this is God speaking, not some impostor. The believer knows that God wishes us to accept them as true because He guarantees their truth. Sometimes he also sees that they contain no flaw or contradiction that would make them unreasonable. Often he is aware of implied unselfish obligations if he is to live consistently with the principles of faith. When the person yields to God revealing, he is at least as intelligent as a newspaper reader who accepts the news from a reliable reporter or as prudent as a telephone subscriber who accepts the word of the company's editors about the spelling of a friend's name or his address in the telephone book.

Such an act of belief is a compliment to God. It honors His knowledge and respects His truthfulness. It is an act of obedience to God's orders that we believe what He declares to us. It is a sacrifice to God.[86] It overcomes one's fears of the duties involved in the new supernatural life of faith. It trusts God's provident way of teaching us, according to our social nature, through accredited witnesses and teachers of His past revelations. Faith is an act worthy of a loving child of God who appreciates the loving instructions and loving gifts of our Father in heaven. To believe is to begin to do the will of our heavenly Father. Naturally, the Father's approval and rewards will follow.

Since the only decisive motive for free assent is the authority of God revealing the truth, genuine faith accepts all that God has revealed. Faith does not finically look for "sweet and pleasing" truths. Heresy chooses among revealed truths; orthodoxy generously welcomes the whole body of faith. We may emphasize at Easter the truth of Christ's resurrection and the associated truths of His divinity, the success of His redemption, our own destiny to heaven, and our coming bodily resurrection. We truly choose to believe these truths; but we do not choose them and reject other truths. Our Credo at Easter is a total acceptance of all that God has revealed.

TRIUMPHANT FAITH

The Gloria is the song of joy at Christmas. The Credo is the victory chant at Easter. Faith is the paschal beatitude, for a blessing has been pronounced on believers. What, we ask, is this victory or prize which God awards for belief?

In one important respect the recorded statement of the beatitude on belief differs from the earlier eight beatitudes. To each of those others some explicit spiritual reward is attached; here no reward is immediately mentioned.[87] For instance, the poor in spirit, whose hearts have given up earthly riches, are promised instead the kingdom of heaven. The omission in the instance of believers can readily be supplied from the rewards assigned to faith by Jesus in His mortal lifetime and by Saints John, Peter, and Paul. We may complete our Lord's statement to Thomas by saying: Blessed are those who, though they have not seen, do believe *because they shall have eternal life*. Our Master taught this in His sermon on the Bread of Life: "He who believes is in possession of eternal life."[88] St. Peter encourages the persecuted Christians to hold on to their faith, loving Him whom they have not seen, because the reward of faith is the salvation of their souls.[89] St. John tells us that he recorded the Resurrection that we might believe that Jesus is the Messias, the Son of God, and that through belief we might have life in His name.[90] Blending thoughts on faith and charity, John writes in his first epistle:

> This is the victory that has conquered the world, our faith. Now, who is it that is a victor over the world, if not he that believes that Jesus is the Son of God? He it is who came to make us victors by purifying and redeeming us, and by the effusion of the Spirit. . . . I write this to you, that you, believing as you do in the name of the Son of God, may know that you have eternal life.[91]

The life of vision is the reward; faith is the preliminary qualifying test.

Mindful of this connection between faith and the life of vision, the Church asks the candidate for baptism: "What do you ask of God's Church?" When he answers, "Faith," she asks further: "What does faith lead you to?" The candidate answers, "To life everlasting."[92]

Faith is, then, the victory of Christ, the Light of the World. Easter, the day of victory, is a special feast of light, of the Light given to the faithful, who are the people *full of faith* in the Light that escaped from the dark grave. The wisest thing in the world is faith in one who rose from the grave as He said. The tips of light moving through the church on the Easter Vigil when the candles answer the three cries of *Lumen Christi*[93] remind us of the waves of courage that today are spreading the truth

of the risen Christ throughout the world. The missionaries to unbelievers near and far, the rural pastors building
up the number of Christ's faithful, the martyrs in whom
faith glows in crimson colors, parents at home, and teachers in Catholic institutions are proclaiming Christ.

Surely, we must pray at Easter to cherish the faith and,
like Paul and Patrick, to have the right to sum up our
lives in the victorious words:

"I have kept the faith!"[94]

10. THE GRACE OF CHRIST'S FRIENDSHIP

JESUS APPEARS

The Saviour set the tone for His Easter visits when He instructed the holy women and Mary Magdalene to tell "My brethren" about His rising.[95] He had raised them to the status of friends at the Last Supper. To Him they are His brethren, despite their recent failures. The record of the forty days charmingly displays His friendship for them.

Each visit is a friend's loving act in the freedom of His coming, in the motive of the apparition, and in the varied personal manner of His approach to different characters.

Thoughtfully and patiently He tried to get them ready for the sight of Him by visions of angels, messages, and provocative conversations with Himself in disguise. Yet His visits always surprised them. For the actual moment and manner of His coming was always unannounced. He chose whom He would visit, when and how soon He would come and how long He would stay, where He would see them, how He would greet them, and how much of His person and mind He would make known to them. Though they might seek Him at the grave or in the garden of burial, He came when He saw fit, following no apparent schedule or pattern in His comings and goings. But He always knew where to find them when He and they were ready for each other.

One feature marks all these visits. All of them are to His former friends, none of them to His enemies.[96] These are days to gladden His friends, not to judge His enemies. These are days to strengthen His future witnesses, not to silence His critics. For that matter, His persecutors are terror-stricken enough by the guards' reports of the wide-open tomb and its missing captive. There is a usual priority of earlier visits to those friends who stood by the cross and mourned at His grave. Surely He made unreported calls on the two Jews who had given Him noble burial.

Love for them determined His purposes in coming. True, His own soul was gladdened by their delight in Him. But as comforter of souls, He was bringing the glad news and radiant sight of His glory so that they might share His joy, pick up heart, receive more of His gifts, and exult in His victory for their sakes. He would spend His first days of glory in doing good for them on earth. Thus He would lead them to some insight into His activities for them in heaven. Before His sufferings and separation from them, He had promised them a joy which no one could ever take away and a rich reward if they would suffer with Him.[97] True friend that He is, He is making a first payment on this happiness of His friends. For each of them that first wonderful meeting with the risen Lord was life's most heart-firing experience. It is not only the Shepherd who has come back to His scattered flock and the Master to His followers; it is the Friend who is re-united in love with His best friends.

Other major aims of His apparitions were to make them convinced and persevering witnesses to His Resurrection and teachings, to confer fuller priestly powers, to form them in their apostolic functions, and to fit their souls for the coming of the Holy Spirit in the near future.[98] In accomplishing these purposes, Christ's grace grew in them; for the spiritual life in them, as in us, is a pro-gressive participation in Christ's Resurrection and in the charity of the divine Friend.

Upon returning, He is most concerned to show the un-failing sweetness of His friendship. His crucifixion had crushed their worldly ambitions of sharing temporal rule with Him; His defeat had disheartened them; His danger had made some of them hide. Yet the cunning propaganda of the Pharisees and the stunning miscarriage of justice had not changed their appreciation of His holiness and goodness to them. He readily forgave them, for He knew they grieved much and He was their friend. If anything, His friendship now seems warmer, as though the lonely grief of His Passion has shown Him by experience the human need of friendly comfort. If anything, His friend-ship now is more beyond challenge than it used to be, for who can question His personal love after He has laid down His life for His friends?

Jesus' first glance at each of His friends was itself a

thrilling grace. What winning gladness, what personal interest, what transforming sunlight in those peaceful, magnetic eyes! His look awakened the other's powers, healed fear and mistrust, and wooed a return of love. Like the gaze of God on the first fresh morning of creation, Christ's face was creative and redemptive.

His greeting words to each show how well He knows them. He calls Magdalene, Peter, Thomas, and Paul by name. He speaks to Magdalene with tenderness and urges restraint on her impulsive affection. He wishes peace to the Apostles and scolds them a bit for their unbelief; but this, too, was characteristic of Him. To Cleophas and his companion He spoke like a wise rabbi to scholarly Jews. With Thomas, He takes the part of a strong leader who must win back a noble, stubborn, and dispirited soldier. Immediately after the miraculous catch of fish, He gladly served the seven their morning breakfast on a sandy beach. From Peter He evokes a triple heroic profession of loyal love. When He calls Paul, He rebukes him for resisting grace, He overpowers his powerful personality and knocks him from his mount, and He identifies Himself with His persecuted Church for the sake of this future apostle of His love for His mystical body. Paul learned from Christ his own genius for friendship: "to be all things to all men."[99]

Any mark of true friendship that philosophers have tabulated shines in Christ: nearness to His beloved ones, conversation, helping, gifts, sharing work and activities, union in sorrow and in joy, forgiving, preparing and promising endless future gifts, oneness in mind and will, unselfish pursuit of the good of the beloved, mutual knowledge of the friendship — all the thoughts, hopes, deeds, and prospects of friendship are here. His gifts fill our lives like blossoms hanging on May boughs, but the best is always the gift of Himself. Of this gift, St. Thomas in his *Verbum supernum* sings:

> He gave — Himself
> At His birth, for our companion,
> At the Supper, for our food,
> By His death, for our price,
> In His kingdom, for our crown.

CHRIST DWELLING IN YOUR HEARTS

For us, too, Easter is a festival of the Friend who comforts us. The generous friendship which the Apostles knew belongs to all of us who have His sanctifying grace. As friends, we should be glad of the glorious gladness of our risen Friend. We should beg for more of this friendship as a proof of His paschal victory in us. St. Paul prayed that his Ephesians might possess this amazing friendship:

> I beseech the Father . . . that he may grant you, in keeping with his glorious riches, to be strengthened with power through the Spirit for the development of your inner selves, and to have Christ dwelling through faith in your hearts, and to be rooted and grounded in love. Thus will you have power to grasp fully . . . the breadth and length and height and depth of this mystery [of our salvation] and to know Christ's love which surpasses knowing.[100]

How shall Christ dwell in our hearts? How shall we, with His grace, be genuine friends of so tremendous a lover? We must learn and practice all the arts of true friendship in our dealings with Him. We must keep Him alive in our thoughts, cherish memories of Him in our imagination, deepen our understanding of Him by growing faith, sweeten our lips with His name, do His will by sinless obedience. To love Him we must keep His commandments,[101] stand fast when He asks us to carry His cross, and selflessly love His other friends in His Church.

We are familiar with the paradox of the exchange of
Christ's death for our life. But St. Paul who knew Christ's
friendship well tells us that there is more to it than just
benefiting from a friend's death for us. "Christ died for
all, in order that they who are alive may live no longer
for themselves, but for him who died for them and rose
again."[102]

A life that combines keen yearning for Him and joyous
giving to Him can be the only response worthy of so
boundless a friendship. A life that seeks to please Him
always, to love Him ever more purely, to be totally loyal
to him even unto death is the right life of a friend of
Christ. It is the lover's supreme interest that Christ live
in him and that he live, die, and reign with Christ.[103]

OUR MEETINGS WITH JESUS

Since we are His chosen friends, He comes to visit us
during our lifetime. It is an everlasting surprise that He
should care enough for us to come. He plans His calls;
we never fall in with Him by accident; He runs into us by
the ingenious devisings of His love. He comes only in
faith, not in vision. But it is truly He, the risen Lord.

His favorite times for coming seem to be when we are
seeking Him in prayer, when we consult Him in the decisions of conscience, when we are bearing some crosses and
mourning with Him, when we are helping needy friends
of His, when He absolves our sins, when we heed His
voice in our superiors, and when He comes in His hidden
physical humanity in our Holy Communions.

May we ever be glad to meet Him whenever He comes.
We learn from His friends at Easter some excellent greet-
ings to our Friend. "Rabbouni." "My Lord and my God."
"It is the Lord." "Lord, You know that I really love You."

"Please, be our guest." "Come, Lord Jesus."[104] Or maybe we prefer Mary His Mother's single joyful word: "Jesus."

We have two more important appointments to meet Jesus, person to person. We await His coming at the hour of our death. Those who are His friends are glad to have Him come for them, even at that hour of justice. "How sweet it is to die," writes St. Margaret Mary, "after being constantly devoted to the Sacred Heart" of our Judge.[105] The second coming brings Him to purgatory to call us to His kingdom and to see Him face to face. We await most eagerly that coming of the eternal Friend. Come, come, Lord Jesus. We wish to see and touch Your wounds. We wish to rest in Your Heart. We wish to begin our never-ending Easter with a glad welcome to You: "I see the Lord. Alleluia! I love my Lord. Alleluia!"

11. THE GRACE OF DIVINE CARE

THE MYSTERY OF THE CROSS

If radio stations on Easter Sunday could broadcast a tape recording of the explanation of the Passion which Christ gave to Cleophas and his companion, we listeners would hear the most brilliant of all lectures on the Scriptures. Those two travelers to Emmaus, though minor witnesses of the Resurrection, received a special favor. The Lord's conversation with them portrays Him as teacher and comforter of the mind. The Gospels elsewhere indicate that a major activity of His golden forty days was to teach the Apostles the plan of salvation in which His dying and rising are bound together.

Walking with these two disciples along that brown country road, Christ sympathized with their grief, their perplexity about His tragic end, and their bewilderment over the rumor of His resurrection. He spoke to them as an unknown, kindly, well-read rabbi who respected their knowledge of their own holy books and their sincere desire to understand the ways of God. He based His argument on the words of the prophets and on the symbolic types of Christ mentioned in their books. His conclusion was that, given the divine certainty of these predictions, "the Messias should undergo these sufferings and thus enter into his glory."[106] St. Luke mentions that He interpreted for them every passage in the sacred writings which spoke of Himself, but the passages from Isaiah, Zachariah, David, Malachi, and Micah about His Passion and glory must have received fuller comment.

The rich details of David's twenty-first psalm, quoted on the Cross, and of Isaiah's description of the suffering servant were almost photographs of the future. The group of prophets had foretold that the Messias, descendant of David, was to live when temporal power had passed into alien hands. A victim of great injustice which He bore with noble sweetness, He would be sold for thirty pieces of silver, rejected by His own people, slapped, scourged, spit upon, nailed between criminals, blasphemed during His tortures. The garments of this outcast would be divided by lot. He would drink vinegar, and His heart would be pierced. But the seers had also foreknown that God would not let corruption touch His dead body and that His sepulcher would be glorious. His new clean sacrifice according to the manner of Melchisedech would take the place of the old Hebraic offerings.[107] His Church, too, succeeding the temple and synagogue, would have a glorious career. Jesus would have here cleared up misunderstandings about the temporal realm which Jewish imagination had read into the Messianic paeans about the Church and her spiritual blessings.

He also reminded the two walking beside Him of the Messianic types: the paschal lamb, the serpent raised to save the people, Melchisedech, and Jonas. His words flooded their minds with insight into the prophetic texts and the divine plan of salvation; and He burnt their hearts, as He so well could, with love and rejoicing. Though they had heard and read these Scriptures hundreds of times, they had understood very little. Now they all fitted together; the secrets were uncovered; the total trend and related meaning shone before their minds. It was stunning. It was true. The Messias, though He is the royal Son of God, must follow the divine plan; He must suffer and die, and only then must win by rising. The pair had not seen Him risen, but they now were ready to take the holy women's reports at full value.

The heavenly Teacher may have gone further with these intent listeners who still had not detected His identity. Had their crucified Master ever suspected or predicted His own sufferings or glory? If He were the Messias, He would have known the sense of the prophecies about Himself. Cleophas and his partner began to remember one after another unbelievable hints about His scourging and crucifixion and those mysterious remarks about the sign of Jonas and His rebuilding of the Temple in three days. Yes, Christ had clearly foreseen all the majestic providence of God in His regard.

Perhaps their Counselor went on to show the wisdom of this design of redeeming men through the Son's death and resurrection. First, the wisdom of His death. This surely showed Him to be true, mortal man. It proved again His deep sympathy with all sufferers and His readiness to share the common human lot. His willing death revealed the boundless love He had for men and the precious value of grace and heaven. It magnificently honored the justice of God who demanded so great a sacrifice from so holy a Redeemer to undo human guilt and to restore men to His favor. It fitted in perfectly with the Hebrew conception of sacrificial salvation through a victim's blood. It unmasked the hideous and ruthless hatred of the powers of evil for all that is good since Satan for a day had dared to crush the one perfect man, the Son of God made man. The depth of His humiliation and pain, motivated by loving obedience to God, measured the coming greatness of the glory that God would heap on Him. Moreover, this example of heroism made sense as the proper thing for this teacher of the value of suffering and for this leader who demanded cross-bearing from His followers.

Their Companion spoke next of the wisdom of His rising. It proved that God was on His side, pleased with His sacrifice and miraculously sealing His teachings. It proved His own godhead. It indicated the fabulous splendor of His reward. It gave hope to all His followers, even in their bitterest sufferings and martyrdoms. It defeated Satan by the wood through which Satan had defeated Adam, God's image.[108] It won for Him the holy kingdom of His Church.

In some such way the Traveler unfolded to them God's plan and will for human salvation. The continuity of Christ's life and death with the centuries-old history of the Hebrews, the total richness and brilliant wisdom of it, so worthy of God, swept all misgiving from them. The beauty and generosity of the divine intentions and government thrilled every recess of their souls. They gladly urged Him to be their guest for dinner and the night. His reward for their appreciative listening and their courteous invitation was the vision of Himself alive, risen, glorious, in the moment when He broke bread.

THE RELIGION OF CROSS AND CROWN

For full faith and strong hope we need to understand the whole doctrine of Christ about the cross. He does not merely teach a doctrine of enduring trouble and resigning ourselves to God's permission of evil. Nor does He merely teach the actuality of coming relief in the Resurrection. He teaches the connection between the two, of suffering as the means and of glory as the end, of dying for the sake of ever living, and of the love of God binding the mortal and immortal states of man into a unity. The Passion, alone, would make no sense and would shock us as a tragic crime. The Resurrection, alone, would reveal divine power but would be an unearned bounty. But in Christ's doctrine, pain and glory are tied together as inseparable elements of His own life and of every Christian's adventure of saving his soul. The Man of Sorrows is destined to joy. The Cross-bearer is destined to wear the glorious wounds. Similarly, all who follow Christ must fight sin, but the painful fight will end in victory. Hardship must earn one's reward; but the price is worth the certain prize.

This is the doctrine of the eighth beatitude. "Blessed are the victims of persecution for conscience' sake, for theirs is the kingdom of heaven. Blessed are you when you are reviled, or persecuted, or made a target for nothing but malicious lies — for my sake. Rejoice; yea, leap for joy; a rich reward awaits you in heaven."[109]

This is the doctrine of the wheat grain that first must die beneath the soil, break its seed coat, lose itself, and then rise up, not alone, but in a fruitful multiplication of its original self.[110] The decorative Easter lilies remind us of their start as tiny bulbs buried in ground, hidden, bursting their casing, cared for by God, and reaching upward to a glory beyond that of Solomon's rich attire. It is the sequence of death and burial before the new rising from the earth, of loss of life before finding fuller life, of dying to self and its disorders before rising in union with Christ. The narrow, self-protecting, isolating bounds of self must be escaped; for these limit our love of God and of our fellow men.

The demand of Christ that we take up a daily cross behind Him may make us wince.[111] But if He should spare us pain of body and humiliation of spirit and the uncertainties of battle for His love, He would also deprive us of nearness to Himself, of sharing with Him in helping others, and of our own greater rewards. Charity, not complacent magnanimity, not stoic calm, is what the Christian must have to walk with Christ into glory. And suffering, as a simple matter of fact, is one of the greatest tests of love for God and for God's children. The road of the cross is not a rutted backwoods lane leading nowhere; it, and it alone, is the King's own highway to triumph.

Therefore, Paul and Peter in their letters come back to this theme of the divine plan that unites death and life.[112] The true disciple of Christ must accept this divine doctrine, heed the divine invitation to take up the cross, and follow the divine example of gentle patience and forgiving love during his suffering. He is never surprised or dejected by the attack of the cross on his selfishness. He is contented to bear it. He comes even to give thanks for it as a precious gift and rejoices in it. Some saints pray for and choose sufferings in order to identify themselves more with their beloved Saviour. Most of all, the true disciple never fails in confidence that the divinely assigned cross will have its reward. He knows he will reach the divine light by the dark cross: *per crucem ad lucem.*

CONFIDENCE IN THE FAITHFUL SHEPHERD

Hope, flowering from faith, is a high honor which we must pay our Redeemer.

The Church has chosen the Good Shepherd as the theme of the liturgy for the second Sunday after Easter; for His Passion proved His boast of fidelity to death, and the new converts are invited to loving trust in following their Shepherd.[113] A favorite greeting card presents the risen Good Shepherd, wreathed in glory, walking along a grassy crest, His crook adorned with a cross, and His lambs trailing behind with faces upturned to Him.

This Shepherd is the faithful Heart in whom we should trust with all our heart. He knows His own; He has laid down His life for His own; He has come back to life for their sake; He is to be ever with them to the end of the world. He has foreseen and provided for their every spiritual need. He does not fail to arrange for those temporal needs which are essential to the soul's salvation. He is ever near us, His eyes ever watchful, His voice ever calling, His shoulders ever ready to carry the wounded, His arms beating off every enemy, His heart ever giving new care. The Lord Christ is my Shepherd,[114] I have no reason to be troubled.

To gain confidence in Him, we must reflect, pray, and act.

We reflect on the strong reasons for hopefulness. Such considerations include our knowledge of God's power, promises, and love; our certainty of His all-foreseeing, all-wise, all-good government of us; our belief in the merits and success of our Saviour; our memories of God's past kindnesses; our assurance of His forgiveness of past sins; the guarantees supporting Christ's many promises. He who rose as He said can do anything which His honor and love wish to do for us.

We pray for confidence in God and in Christ, in Providence and the Sacred Heart. For confidence is a gift of grace and, therefore, needs prayer to win it.

We act. We repress moods, images, feelings of unfounded discontent, pointless worries, and exaggerations of our troubles. When we meet setbacks, we rebound. We cultivate appreciative and grateful attitudes. We turn our minds to the grounds for confidence; we make acts of hope again and again; we use the means which God provides for our well-being. We give thanks when we are permitted to assist Christ in His sufferings. Like a bride deeply in love, we trust ourselves, our future, and our happiness to God's love. Love trusts the Beloved.

I hope in the Lord, said the Psalmist, I cannot miss.[115] I am His sheep; I need but follow my Shepherd. I may walk with Him, as Cleophas did, while He awakens my confidence and prepares me for the moment when He will show His living glory to my eyes.

12. THE GRACE OF A GARDEN

His Body Laid in a Garden

Joseph of Arimathea offered his own new tomb for the
deceased Jesus, and it was in a garden hard by Calvary.[116]
One wonders why the Holy Spirit and St. John mentioned
this garden in their memoirs of the crucified and risen
Saviour.

The reason must lie in the fitness of the situation and
in the mission of the Redeemer. The first Adam had
sinned in a garden. Expelled from it, he no longer took

a daily walk with God and lost much of the former beauty of his daily life. But as he set out for the fields, deserts, and mines of earth, he heard the promise of a Redeemer. It was fitting that this Redeemer should fulfill that promise in a garden and there bring back to man much of that lost beauty. It was right that God's new friendship with man should be shown in the Son's garden meeting with His dear Magdalene. Moreover, the happiness that beauty can bring the heart also belonged to the human heart of Christ on the morning of His recovery of life. He had always loved nature and the living outdoors, and spoke feelingly of its lilies and birds. He can see and hear them on this morning of glory.

In the distant future He shall return to earth as lordly Judge in power and majesty; but today at redemption's dawn, He appears in loving kindness and loveliest beauty. This royal anointing of beauty in His risen Form was well deserved for His endurance of the humble ugliness of "the worm" and "the leper" during the hours of the Passion.

The Christian sense of beauty recalls that closed paradise of the golden age of our first parents when nature and grace were in perfect harmony and sin had despoiled us of none of the beauties of the soul, the body, or the external world. Christian imagination remembers how much mention there is of gardens and flowers in that Canticle of Canticles which presents Christ consorting with His bride, the soul. It also looks forward to heaven as a garden universe; for Christ told the thief that His kingdom was a garden, and St. John saw the tree of life and living waters in the City of the Lamb.[117] Christian intelligence knows that God is Beauty and the Creator of the shining goodness of things and that He has made people and things beautiful to show that this world is a lover's invention and gift, not just an efficient engineer's serviceable drab machine. Perhaps another reason for the beauty of our little earth is the divine wish to make it a worthier place for the temporal life of God's Son and His friends. Surely, only God has put this delight in beauty and this craving for it into our powers. He means it as one more way of pulling us to Himself. Why else, too, is beauty so prominent an element of His Son's religion?

Suburban living and recent home architecture have sharpened our interest in the human meanings, possibilities, and uses of gardens.

Gardens are a favorite portion of our homes, outdoor extensions of our family dwellings. They are places for the recreational, relaxed aspects of our after-duty living. They make yards for the children's safe playing. Here we entertain dearer friends and pursue a number of our hobbies and take some healthy exercise in pleasant weather under the open sky. They are quiet spots, set back from street traffic and protecting the enclosed house from bordering property lines. Thus they give spaciousness, freedom, and privacy, as well as better setting to a house. In them we escape from confining walls and close pressures and tiresome formalities. They are places of sunlight and beauty, where restful greenery meets the eye, where growing flowers of many hues and shapes bring us the special treasures of the changing seasons, where birds are welcome to sing and feed, and where our fancies play freely, according to our own tastes, in irregular arrangements of flower beds and walks, in building fountains and miniature waterfalls and bridges over lily ponds, and in setting about nonsensical toys for the delight of little ones. Those considerations of utility, of saving space and costs, and of the streamlined regularity which mark offices and shops are seldom thought of in gardening. These gardens are the places for variety, beauty, surprise; a place for living things, for picnicking, for enjoying life. Gardens are a bit of heaven encircling our own homes. And as love delights in adorning the beloved and desires heart's ease alone with the beloved, gardens with their beauty and privacy and friendliness are famous in literature as the meeting place of lovers.

So, Christ, Himself beautiful and loving beautiful things and desiring to win us by His physical and spiritual beauty, rose to life in a garden. This event happened in early spring when the mysterious beauty of resurgent blossoming bursts forth after the dreary days of late winter. St. Paul calls the risen Lord the first-fruits of the dead, and this suggests comparing Christ with the first flowers, the new buds, and the fresh birdsongs of spring. The attractive beauties of any healthy adult face, human voice and organism far excel other bodily beauties; and how much the beauty of the Flower which is Christ's glorified body excels all other human beauties. St. Paul adds his own special touch to describe the beauty of Christ under the familiar metaphor of light: I herald, he says,

> the gospel which proclaims to them the splendor of Christ, who is God's image. . . . The God who said, "Let light shine from the midst of darkness," has shone in our hearts, to give enlightenment through the knowledge of God's glory, glowing in the face of Christ.[118]

The Splendor of God: the light glowing in the face of Christ. It makes us wonder how God may be using the heart-burning beauties of nature and of our faith to teach us more of His love and to bring us closer to Himself. Surely, we are aware that the most shining beauties of people on earth are but delicate shadows of the heart-gladdening beauty which God is perfecting for those who love Him.

Where Lovers Meet

Considering all these associations with gardens in Christ's
and our minds, we find it almost to be expected that two
devoted friends, the God-Man in His immortal splendor
and Mary Magdalene in her fragile penitent beauty, should
have met in the garden on the morning of the Resurrection. Here He found the selfless and total love which had
led Him to come from paradise. He asked her, as the
angels had, "Good woman, why are you weeping?" Because
of her own obscuring tears and her frantic preoccupation
with finding His dead body, she thought that this living
man might be a gardener or caretaker for Arimathea, only
a stranger who might supply some clue. What an entrancing surprise! The stranger was her best friend; the dead
man was this living One. Their mutual cries of recognition
— Miriam! Rabbouni! — outsang all the melodies of the
birds that morning.[119] As the angelic Gloria set the whole
world singing Christmas carols, so these two joyful voices
started all our Easter alleluias.

At that, Mary Magdalene was not far wrong in thinking
Him to be a gardener. He is a heaven-sent gardener, a
caretaker of the lovely life of grace, a gardener of souls,
and the owner of the Garden of Paradise. All seed, growth,
and fruit of the spirit are His doing. He is the Sower, the
Laborer, and the Harvester. He digs, plants, waters, sprays,
cultivates, prunes, and labors day and night for the moral
beauty of human souls. Today He is making our souls
lovely and hereafter He will let the beauty of grace within
us transform our flesh when we rise like straight giant lilies
to share His risen comeliness. The angels might well envy
risen men for having bodies in which they mirror the
beauty of the risen Christ.

Christians surround their dear resting dead with stately

parks. This is not a mere pagan effort to soften the harsh-
ness of ugly death. We remember that Christ's Mother
laid His dead body in a vault in a garden, and we expect
our brethren to rise with the just to beauty in this very
burial ground. What sweetness melts a heart when it
thinks of the divine Gardener in all His radiance smiling
on the glittering beauty of the bodies of His redeemed.
In that hour we will clearly understand that human life
is a comedy, not a tragedy after all. With all its ups and
downs and after the stark interlude of death, man's way
on earth reveals a perfect purpose and closes with a happy
ending. This happy ending, planned by God and merited
by Christ, makes life truly a divine comedy and a symbol
of redemption and resurrection.

The Good Fragrance of Christ

What can we do to copy Christ by making Easter a
festival of beauty? It is not enough to heap flowers on our
altars and baptismal fonts, to decorate our homes with
bright blooms in Christ's honor, and to array our bodies in
gaily-colored garments. What do we do to make our souls
beautiful for Christ? Do we invite Him to plant and labor
within us at His discretion? Do we copy Magdalene in
spreading the beauty of Christ and the happiness of the
Resurrection to others? The good example of our virtues
and works of faith is the perfume spreading abroad the
knowledge of Christ, the fragrance drawing souls to new
life, as the Apostle informed the Corinthians.[120] Whether
he referred to the perfume of spiced incense or to the scent
of flowers matters little. We must lure souls to Christ, the
Bud of Mary, the Mystical Rose. Loving according to our
faith in the risen Saviour does win people to our Lord. It
announces the news of His victory. Most of us need to

talk little; but all must live Christ fully. Then men will
see the moral beauty of Christ, not in Christ, but in us
who belong to Christ. It is quite unnecessary consciously
to aim at giving good example. We need only be first-class
Catholics and then we shall be preaching Christ by living
with and for Christ. Thus we shall be scattering everywhere the sweet aroma of the Resurrection.

The King of Beauty will not forget this service to Him.
He will so well nourish our souls that they will bloom with
graces more profusely than a flowering cherry tree in high
spring. And He will send His angels to escort us into the
garden where He and His Father — our Father, too — shall
garland us with glory and converse with us under the
towering tree of eternal life.[121]

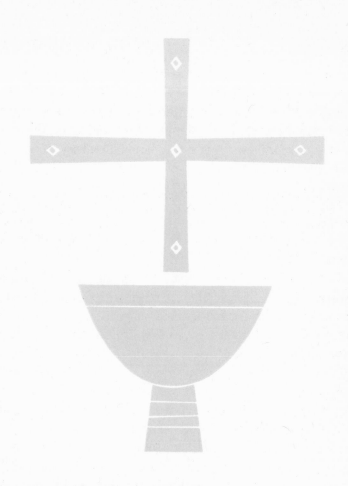

13. THE GRACE OF SIGNS

Every Gospel, especially St. John's, often speaks of the signs and proofs of our blessed Lord's majestic claims for His person and His doctrines.

Early in His Judean preaching, the wonder-working and already popular Christ ran headlong into the hostility of Scribes and Pharisees. When His astonishing cures and routing of devils, His claims to forgive sins and to be Master of the Sabbath, and His reproof of their mean-spirited religious attitudes had provoked them, they snarled a challenge to Him to give them a visible proof of His claims. They insincerely ignored the many miracles He had already worked and the glorious sanctity of His life. Yet He met them by a most daring prophecy of an incredible coming miracle.

> A headstrong and adulterous* generation demands a proof of my claims! But a proof will not be given it except the proof which Jonas gave: just as Jonas spent three days and three nights in the belly of the sea monster, so the Son of Man will spend three days and three nights in the heart of the earth.[122]

He repeated this same appeal to the sign of Jonas later when they asked Him to show them a sign in the skies to support His claims. He ignored so puerile a sign of their own choice and again referred them to the divinely chosen and greater sign of His Resurrection.[123] If they could read the indications of fine and stormy weather, their knowledge of Hebrew lore and their curiosity about the intriguing miracle done on Jonas would give them insight into the relation between Jonas and Himself.

He announced a multiple comparison between Jonas and the Son of Man. On the one hand, the sea giant's interior, on the other, the tomb; the body of the prophet to Nineve hidden in the monster, the dead body of Christ buried in the ground; no corruption in the body of either; the interval of three days in both instances; Jonas cast out for the safety of the sailors, Christ rejected for the salvation of all men; the return of the living Jonas to shore and the return of Christ to life on earth.

Christ predicted the same future event as testifying to His powers under a different metaphor when He whipped the money-changers from the Temple. In fury, they demanded what was His right to act so. Knowing His

---

* Adulterous, i.e., unfaithful to the covenant of love and service of God.

Father's presence in the Temple and in His own human nature, He retorted while probably pointing to Himself: "If you destroy this sanctuary, I will build it up again in three days." They jeered, reminding Him that it had taken forty-six years to build the Temple.[124] Yet they and their coached false witnesses remembered this defiant answer later when they tried Him and when they asked Pilate to guard the tomb. It is noteworthy both that Jesus says "I" will rebuild it, by His divine nature, of course, and that He again declares an outside limit of three days.

As He suffered, seemingly powerless, on the cross, they ridiculed His former miraculous gifts and suggested that He now show Himself the Messias by coming down from the gibbet.[125] But He would give them no cheap sign like escaping from pain. He would die and then come up from the grave. That greatest of wonders, fulfilling the most improbable of prophecies, would be an infinitely greater proof. His own bodily resurrection on a definitely forecast day would be the ultimate test on which He staked His teachings and cause, His claims to be from God and to be God. All His other wonders, however plentiful and evident they were, He would forego and would risk all on the Resurrection.

Learned Hebrews and even the ordinary people habitually regarded miracles and verified prophecies as sure proofs of God's action and of God's approval of anyone who asserted that He was speaking or acting in God's name. For God alone can predict free future events with certainty of detail; His omniscience makes this possible. And God alone can freely and powerfully surpass the powers of nature and control human liberty by His governing omnipotence. If the miracle occurs or the prediction comes true, it is a sure sign of God's action and of God's signature on the wonder-worker and his message.

God cannot be a witness to a fraud and will not lead His people into error by approving impostors.

A sign is itself observed and also leads its observer to knowledge of something behind the sign. Flags are signs of nations and patriotism; words are signs of thought; wedding rings are signs of nuptial troth. Just as one's signature is a sign of the writer and his acceptance of the contract or paper, so miracles are God's signature on religious claims. God speaks through His commissioned teacher and God manifests that the commission is divine in source by genuine miracles and by prophecies made and come true.

So, these concrete facts — the risen Christ, the open tomb, and His discarded grave clothes — are all signs of a great physical miracle wrought on a certainly dead man; they fulfill a great prophecy made by an older prophet and by Christ. They lead us to certainty that Christ is a teacher and ambassador sent by God, that His claims to be the Messias and the Son of God are true, and that His asserted powers of forgiving sins, of establishing a new religion, of judging mankind, and of redeeming our race are all authentic. The justification of these claims can be the only reasonable meaning to be read into the signs. God loves and approves Him and bids us listen to Him and believe what He says and do what He commands. In raising up the dead Christ, God spoke a miraculous word in favor of His Word, His religion, and His doctrines.

The angels at the open sepulcher seem to have been amazed at the unbelief, dismay, and total surprise of the holy women and of Magdalene. He is risen, just as He foretold. Didn't you expect it? It's the third day. Of course, He's alive. He has just kept His prophetic promise. You believed Him to be the Son of God. Well, this is God's work. Of course, He is risen, He is not here in the place of the dead. Seek Him alive.[126] Life is His sign.

The popular medieval mystery, *The Visit to the Sepulcher*, played in churches and monastic chapels on Easter morning, had several persons act as the holy women who lifted the shroud and other linens from the sepulcher at the altar and displayed these relics to the congregation with the well-loved lines: "Let the Jews either restore the buried one or adore the risen One."[127] Now this clever dilemma a bit confuses motives of believability with motives of belief. It is a big step from concluding that the Resurrection is a fact and that the words of the risen One are credible to the assent of faith by which one believes the truth of all His words. No one can reach faith by playing the shrewd detective who traces all the clues, examines all the interested parties, asks why no one produced the missing corpse or arrested the Apostles for grave robbery, weighs all the signs and evidences for the fact that Christ died and rose again, and decides that only God raised Him from the grave; and then instantly, by a process of pure reasoning says, "I believe in the divinity of Christ and in the whole creed which He taught." This rational inquiry leads at best to historical certainty that this man named Jesus Christ died and later lived again. Faith demands something much more, namely, the inner motion of God's grace to make an act of supernatural belief and a new free act of the believer's spiritual powers accepting as true what Christ has taught because He reveals with the authority of God.[128]

There are many motives or signs of the believability of Christ; these are strong credentials of His teaching mission. But the motive for believing His teachings is only the authority of God revealing these truths; and this divine authority over us is twofold: intellectual and moral. The intellectual authority is God's infinite knowledge of all truths, even the hidden, the free, and the future. The

moral authority is founded on God's holiness which speaks
to men only truthfully and, accordingly, deserves assent;
and on His right to our obedience of intellect and of
conduct since He is our Creator, Owner of all our powers
and their acts, our Lawgiver and Governor. If He orders
us to believe His instructions to us, faith is necessary to
honor and please Him.

THE SIGN OF THE FISH

The fish plays an interesting part in the Resurrection
record. On Easter night, our Lord uses His bodily ability
to eat the piece of broiled fish as a sign or proof of His
living corporeal organism.[129] A few weeks later He provides
a haul of one hundred and fifty-three fish for Peter, John,
James, Thomas, Nathanael, and two others who had spent
a whole night working their nets without success. But at
His suggestion from the shore at twilight, they make one
more cast on the right side and instantly make a fabulous
catch.[130] This miracle showed His power over nature. It
indicated His continuing interest in their temporal needs.
It was a blessing on them for obeying His command and
a prediction of His future blessings whenever they, His
fishermen, would be trying to bring men into the nets
of His Church. To John, it was an immediate sign by
which he identified the stranger on the beach as the Lord.

By a lucky coincidence of spelling, the first letter of
the five Greek words for "Jesus Christ, the Son of God,
the Saviour," are the five letters of the Greek noun for
fish, I X Th U S.* The early Greek-speaking Christians
adopted this word for a fish or some drawing of a fish
as their secret symbol for their faith in Jesus. Christ is
the Fish. The joint sign of fishes and loaves of bread was

* ΙΧΘΥΣ.

a special symbol of the Blessed Sacrament. Every fish says
to the alert imagination: Believe; eat; you will have life
in Christ.

Our art has used other animals to symbolize the risen
Christ. The paschal lamb has much scriptural recommenda-
tion. The mythological phoenix which rises from its ashes
becomes a figure for Christ dying and reviving. The butter-
fly succeeding to the castoff cocoon represents Christ
once buried, now free and alive. Peacocks and bees have
often been used for this same mystery.[131]

CHRISTIAN SIGNS

Christianity, being both a supernatural and a social religion, must contain many signs of the supernatural and
use signs as a means of communication among its members. By the system of signs God, the Church, and our
teachers try to show us what grace is doing in our souls,
how to understand religious truths better, and how to
lift our minds from sensible signs to supernatural realities.

In regard to the Easter mysteries, God used the rending
of the Temple veil at the hour of Christ's death as a sign
of the end of the Old Law and of the opening of a new
religious approach to God.[132] Christ uses bread and wine
and consecrating words as a sign of the presence of His
risen body in the Eucharist. On Easter night He chose
the sign of a court as the vehicle of penance and pardon
and peace. In the opinion of St. John Chrysostom and
others, the sign of the Son of Man to appear in the
heavens before the end of the world is a brilliant cross.[133]
Certainly, the Church uses the sacramental of the cross
and crucifix very often in her rites, exorcisms, blessings,
and consecrations of objects. It is not too surprising that
Christ, the great wonder-worker, should have many times

conferred the power of miracles on His Church. Indeed, the life, holiness, and attributes of the Church of Christ are among her great credentials as the continuator of Christ's Incarnation throughout history.[134]

Our Lord called our attention to one sign of the Christian: love for one another, similar to His love for us. Again and again, St. John repeats that this love is the token, the brand, the evidence, the sign that we are Christ's.[135] Charity marks the men and women who have died to self and in whose lives Christ lives and reigns. This is the daily sign that we are leading the risen life with the victorious Christ: a glad and glowing love for Christ and all His brethren.

What can I do, dear Christ, to deepen Your favorite sign in my heart?

14. THE GRACE OF WITNESSING

"You Are the Witnesses of All This"[136]

The sign of the Resurrection must have witnesses who know the facts with certainty and realize the connection of the facts with the claim they signify.

Jesus recognized this need of reliable witnesses who would officially report to others what they knew. Hence, He did not immediately go from His tomb to heaven but appeared a number of times to His friends to confirm them as firsthand witnesses and to commission a selected

group of them to be His ambassadors to souls after He
should have gone to the right hand of His Father.

Many lines in the Gospels present Christ claiming to
be an ambassador sent by God with a message for Jews
and Gentiles. St. John had an especially good grasp of
this issue as his accounts of the Teacher's long battle with
the Jewish leaders and His reports of the delegation given to
the Apostles indicate. It is admirable that the Word Himself should graciously come to speak to us of God and the
divine will for us. At twelve He spent several days in the
Temple school to stir up thought on the Messias. He spoke
of His authority to teach as divine in origin, as a Messianic
sign foretold by Isaias. He claimed that His Father had sent
Him to men, that He spoke only what His Father taught
Him to say, and that His Father was giving testimony to
His doctrines by the power of miracles. He called Himself
the Way, the Truth, the Life; the Bread of Life, for His
doctrines nourished souls; the Light of all the World;
the Sower who had gone out to plant truth in many
soils. He demanded belief in Himself and in His words;
He begged them to believe for the sake of His works if
they would not believe Him, or to believe for the sake
of the prophets. He complimented and rewarded those
who accepted His teachings. He told Pilate that He had
come into the world to give testimony to the truth.
Though the leaders of His countrymen murdered Him for
what He had said and claimed, He would not retract
one word of this testimony. That office of teaching summed
up one major aspect of His vocation as the incarnate
Redeemer.

But before He transferred to a chosen band His own
powers as legate of God's truths, He took at least three
important steps. Before His death He gave them some
field experience in spreading the truth about Himself in

their missions to various villages; after His death, He took
great pains that they become informed, convinced witnesses with personal immediate knowledge of His resurrection. Look at His efforts during His second life to turn
these men, who had known Him well for some years, into
qualified witnesses of the fact of His resurrection and the
fact of His glory in this risen state. His third preparatory
step looked to the long future. He would protect them
from forgetfulness or error in their teaching duties by
the gift of the infallible Spirit of Truth.

With the possible exception of John, they gave very
cautiously their adherence to the truth that He was risen.
Most of them were stolid outdoor workmen, little edu-
cated, unused to thinking on unusual matters, slow to
accommodate their minds to new views, new perspectives,
and new realities. The fact of the Resurrection caught
them by complete surprise; it was too unusual, also too
good to be true, and in a way too humiliating in view of
their recent flight from the cross. He knows, when He
appears, that they are wary of their own observations; they
do not mean to let themselves be taken in by a ghost, by
an illusion of their own fancies and hopes, by any bogus
substitute for the true Christ. "See! It is I myself."[137]
He meets every test that their distinct senses and reason
devise. That He was truly a body He made sure by letting
them touch Him; and truly a human body by their eyes
which simultaneously looked at Him present; the same
body as that of the Christ who had died because of the
identical features and because of those revealing wounds
that lingered in His glory; a living body because He showed
them the familiar acts of a living man who eats broiled
fish, converses with His friends, recognizes each of them,
discusses their doubts, their memories of His Passion, and
the meaning of the prophets. Eventually He also reveals

His divinity and His new glory by His sudden appearances and disappearances, by the miraculously filled nets at Tiberias, and by the splendor of His ascending body.

He had special trouble in convincing Thomas. But that man's bold demand to touch Him inside His wounds only makes him a superior witness to the facts; hearsay would not satisfy this stubborn head.

As soon as He has made them certain of Him, on Easter night itself He takes the decisive step of making them world reporters of what they have just witnessed. "As the Father has made me his ambassador, so I am making you my ambassador."[138] Heretofore, He had often told them that they were to be His successors in this divine ambassadorship; but before tonight they had not known of the Resurrection and could not testify to it. Now the capital piece of evidence for their future preaching is complete. When He meets them on the Galilean mountain, He will further instruct them in this duty and privilege of being His voice before the nations. His last great thought on the fortieth day is of His Church and their witness to Him in Judea and beyond to the rim of the earth.

During their waiting for the Holy Spirit, Peter led the eleven in designating another disciple who had known Christ from the beginning to fill up the post vacated by Judas' apostasy. The lot, directed by the Holy Spirit — for all these witnesses and messengers have a divine call, not a personal seizure of this duty — fell on Matthias, who became the new twelfth Apostle. Later, Christ personally intervened to make Paul the special Apostle of the Gentiles; and Paul is ever keenly conscious that Jesus Christ chose him and commanded him to undertake this office of giving witness to Christ crucified and glorified, for it was surely not his own ambition.

Go, Teach All My Commandments[139]

The primary qualification for any witness in court or elsewhere when giving credit to a wedding, a contract, or an accident is immediate knowledge of facts, persons, statements, and circumstances under his notice. All who had known Christ before and after His resurrection met this standard for giving testimony. But Christ appointed only an inner corps of His disciples, the Apostles, to be His public ambassadors to the world. The holy women and Magdalene testified to His brethren and privately. The Apostles, however, received, in addition to the commission, a power of working miracles in support of their mission and the unfailing instruction and protection of the divine Spirit of Truth.

Their duty to publicize Christ crucified and risen and to announce all that He had taught and commanded began immediately after the divine Wind had whirled round them on Pentecost Sunday. Peter in these early sermons and Paul some years later heavily stressed their own knowledge of the Resurrection. They picked and trained other instructors to help them; they consecrated some specially selected men to be their successors and to serve as the pope and resident bishops with God-given right to teach the faith given by Christ. Through this long chain of living witnesses of what they have learned from their predecessors, the truth of Christianity flows down the ages and moves outward to every nation, neighborhood, and person in the whole world.

Some of the facts of their testimony and many of the doctrines which they preached were committed to writing by the authors of the New Testament and their designated successors. But Christ had chosen living witnesses, people with minds alive with truth and faith, human intellects to capture other intellects for the truth. He made His first witnesses and Apostles the heirs of His whole doctrine, and they passed on the precious inheritance in a living chain. For many reasons Christ did not and would not choose a mere book to enshrine His treasured message. A book's objectivity is not enough to compensate for its many shortcomings when it is compared to a living tradition of dedicated teachers, helped by the Spirit of God.

The life of ambassadorship for Christ remains permanently in the Church as one of the highest ways of imitating Christ and one of the major vocations within the Christian community. The heavenly light shed into the world by the Blessed Trinity through the human speech of Christ has cascaded, undimmed and undiminished, to our own Holy Father and all bishops united with Him in faith. Thank God for the teaching body of His Church; it is one of the finer fruits of Christ's victory through the Cross.

SOIL AND SOWERS TODAY

Faith depends upon hearing, and hearing on teaching. The divine witnesses and teachers may send their voices into the whole world, proclaiming the truth of Christ which dwells within them.[140] But we, too, have something to do; we must listen and, having listened, say to our teachers with Peter's first converts and with the Gentile centurion, "What shall we do?"[141] We are not sterile soil in which the Sower puts His doctrine through His contemporary witnesses, but we are God's field, striving to make ourselves fertile soil for His graces. "He who welcomes any one as my ambassador welcomes me." "He who listens to you listens to me." "He who befriends you befriends me."[142] Or, as St. Paul puts it, commending the Galatians: "You welcomed me as one of God's angels, even as Jesus Christ."[143] That is the open spirit with which we receive encyclicals and orders from the Holy Father and the sermons we hear in our churches and the doctrines we read in approved spiritual books. A steady interest in Catholic theology is an excellent way of listening to Christ and growing in the Faith.

All of us laity have singular opportunities to help Christ and His accredited witnesses sow the good seed of Catholic truth. Our fellow workers, our neighbors, our contemporaries, our children are waiting from us for the word and the example which portray Christ to them. We are not bishops or pastors with an official mandate to teach. We are not missionaries bringing light into infidel darkness. We are not martyrs giving crimson witness to Christ nor virginal penitents testifying by crosses to their love of Christ and His brethren. But many of us are asked by our bishops to share in Catholic Action. Many are commissioned to teach in Catholic institutions. Parents everywhere have a major duty to help Christ by forming Him in their little ones. Every one of us can bear some witness to Christ and make Him better known and loved. We can always show others Christ and talk for Christ by living Christ in His fullness in our own lives. All who live by the faith radiate the splendor of the risen Saviour and shine with that hidden fire which Christ's grace fans within them. When people see the effects of the Resurrection in us, they will begin to take an interest in Him who is the Resurrection and their true Life.

He has promised that, if we confess Him before men, He will speak up for us before His Father in heaven.[144]

Risen Saviour, make our voices and our virtues worthy to give loyal witness to Your truth, Your love, and Your glory.

15. THE GRACE OF THE ROCK AND THE SHEPHERD

THE CORNERSTONE AND THE ROCK

The Gospels suggest no compelling reason why the glorified Christ spent all of forty days in Judea and Galilee. Many Catholics feel that He realized that time was needed to reunite His followers to Himself in the old unity of mind and heart and to rebuild their faith, courage, and enthusiasm after the damage done by their reaction to His Passion. During this period He gave much thought and energy to the structure of His own society, "My

106

Church," as He liked to call it. He prudently followed His own advice to build on living rock which no pressures of rain, floods, and storms could wreck.[145]

Jesus built this house of the living God on two foundations: Himself as the invisible Cornerstone and Peter as the enduring rock. Both are perfect for their purpose of unifying the stones of the whole structure, of firmly maintaining the house, and of strongly resisting all forms of destruction.

During the last week of His mortal life He had picked up a prophecy of David and Isaiah about the cornerstone and told the criticizing Pharisees that He Himself was the stone which the builders had rejected but which God had selected to become the cornerstone.[146] God picks His stones for His own building. God and men had different opinions about Christ's position and value. The Pharisees reject Him, preferring their Old Law and their own interpretation of it. Their stone God rejects and selects Christ as the tested, precious stone, fit to be the cornerstone, firmly fixed in the foundations. The cornerstone unites the side walls, the superstructure and substructure; it marks the basic lines and dimensions of the ground plan; often it designates whose house this is. So Christ unites the members who are the stones of His Church; His own divine Person and work as Redeemer are the main features of the faith; on Him our religion is founded and our salvation grounded; and the whole Church, its doctrines, graces, sacraments, laws, members, and glories are truly and only His. He who rejects Christ as the stone rejects His house also and dashes himself to powder by his opposition.

But our Cornerstone became invisible when He moved to the heavenly Jerusalem. Since the visible Church needs a visible foundation, He selected Simon Peter for this function. This choice fell on him one famous day up in Galilee. Jesus had just inquired of the Apostles what was the people's opinion of the Son of Man. As far as they knew, they replied, the people regarded Him as one or other of the former prophets or as John the Baptist. Jesus then put the question: But who do you say I am? Simon Peter spoke up: "You are the Messias, the Son of the living God." Jesus agreed, and His Heart leaped to hear this first profession of His divinity. Peter's faith was at once rewarded by blessing, praise, a great honor, and a perpetual task for the preservation of the Faith. The Son of God said:

> Blessed are you, Simon, son of Jona. It was my Father in heaven that revealed this to you, and not flesh and blood. And I, in turn, say to you: You are Peter, and upon this rock I will build my Church, and the gates of hell shall not prevail against it. I will give you the keys of the kingdom of heaven, and whatever you bind on earth shall be bound in heaven, and whatever you loose on earth shall be loosed in heaven.[147]

He is not yet the rock, but is to become the rock as soon as the Church is established. He is the one base on which all is to be built and to which all must be united. He is the stable bedrock which is ever firm and which no power of evil can undermine, overturn, or splinter. Moreover, He is the key-bearer of the house of God; the steward and vicar who will open the treasures and the very doors of heaven to believers and repentant sinners, and the judge to declare and relax obligations on earth, assured that his decisions and their effects are ratified in heaven.

Thus the man of faith, the first spokesman of Christ's sonship, becomes the Rock. He is no longer Simon, the son of his father Jona; no longer the fisherman by his own vocational choice. He is a new man with a new function: Christ's Rock.

He did not look much like a rock when he crumbled

under the triple hostile challenge of the highpriest's servants by the fireside. But this was before the Resurrection
and Pentecost, that is, before he actually became the
visible head of the Church. Apart from Christ, he is a
very weak rock. But, with Christ victorious, he is something far greater than his mere human self; he holds supernatural strength. When Christ rose again from the rock
slab on which He lay in the tomb, Peter rose again as the
visible rock. Hence, Peter has an important place in the
record of the forty days when the organization of the
Church is being settled.

The very night of his verbal desertion of Christ he began
to weep in loving contrition. His compassion for Christ
may have been second only to Mary's. But he was too
heartsore to appear near the cross with John. However,
he and John kept in touch with each other and together
hurried to the tomb when the women broke the news that
the Lord was missing from the grave.[148] Sometime that
Easter day Peter saw the Lord, the first of the Apostles
to receive this joyous honor.[149] At this interview, whose
details have not been reported, Jesus and Peter must have
come to a complete understanding. Christ must have insisted that he prove his devotion by resuming the leadership of the band, not by surrendering it for past unworthi-
ness. He sent him to strengthen the others in this newly
discovered truth of His resurrection. Thus Christ's prayer
for him at the Supper is already being answered.[150]

Peter saw the Lord at least six times during Christ's
second life. By the time the Holy Spirit came, the soft
stone of his faith had become an indestructible rock, able
to stand forever as the foundation of Christ's house of
God, His Church. Moreover, since Christ came to teach
and save all men of all times and since Christ promised
His unfailing support and constant presence in His Church

to the end of time, the powers of Peter are perpetual in his true successors, the popes.[151] Each duly elected pope becomes, in turn, the Rock of Christ.

THE GOOD SHEPHERD AND THE NEW SHEPHERD

Once before the Ascension, Peter led a party of seven Apostles on a fishing expedition in their home waters.[152] They caught nothing until they took a tip-off about casting their nets to the right from a man on the twilight beach. When the party had landed their immense haul and had eaten of the breakfast which the Master Himself had made for them, Jesus took Peter for a walk along the shore. During their conversation the Lord turned from the figure of the builder, rock, and house to the image of the Shepherd commissioning another head shepherd to lead and care for His own flock. To qualify as pastor of Christ's own beloved, He must love and serve them because of His love for Christ. Therefore, Jesus three times asks Peter to profess his love, and at each profession deepens the grace of love. In return for his love, Christ gives this great heart two great tasks in proof of love: the first is the charity of service to Christ's fold, and the other is the charity of future martyrdom for Christ and the Church. He is now instructed that he is to be more than the rock and more than the strong voice of faith to weaker brethren. He is to feed and tend the lambs *and* the sheep of the Good Shepherd. He is given general spiritual care of Christ's own. He is to lead them to rich pasture and guard them and toil and die for the whole flock of Christ, for both its new young members and the mature older ones.

Peter well remembered and understood our Lord's own earlier description of Himself as the Good Shepherd.[153]

He saw that the shepherd servant could not be better than the Master Shepherd. He knew the Supreme Shepherd's ideal of serving the sheep, of self-sacrifice, of care for the wandering, of a hard and poor and laborious life, of willingness to die should the sheep be attacked, of faithfulness unto death. Peter's later letters have little of the rush, flame, and dazzle of St. Paul's. Rather they show the heart of a great shepherd of the world-wide flock: a fatherly tone, a wide interest in every class of Christians, tender concern for their sufferings, judicious warnings against heretical teachings and against misinterpreting Paul's letters, a sweet joy in their graces, a serene hope because of Christ's resurrection irradiating their lives and destinies.

The food to which Peter the shepherd leads His lambs and sheep is twofold: the Bread of Life, Christ's full revelation,[154] and Christ Himself in the Eucharistic Bread. To this pasture Peter will lead us, by gentle persuasion when he can, by firm command when he must. And as there is only one God and one Redeemer, so there is only one flock and one supreme shepherd on earth.

Till the world becomes extinct, the leadership of Peter is the leadership of Christ, the authority of the vicar is the kingship of Christ on earth, the food of this shepherd is the food of Christ, the light of Peter is the light of Christ, and the strength of the rock is the might of Christ. The history of the papacy repeats that closing scene in St. John's Gospel: Christ walking with Peter, His new chief shepherd. It is ever the risen Christ who is walking and talking with Peter.

The Resurrections of Rome

One of the few sure prospects for our human future on this planet is the fulfillment of Christ's glowing assurances to Peter and His Church. "The gates of hell shall not prevail against this Rock." "I have prayed for you that your faith never fail." "I am with you all days even to the last days of the world." "Heaven and earth shall pass away, but never My word."[155]

The Rome of the spirit, religious Rome, the society of Christ, the Church under the bishop of Rome, is perpetual. When the flesh of Christ rose to die no more, the mystical body rose with Him to enduring life. Unlike the physical Christ, the mystical body still suffers; for it must be conformed to a cross-bearing Head in its days on earth. The Church is a victim with Christ and for Christ. It is vulnerable, for its members are human; it is unconquerable because the divine life of the risen One courses through it. Strangers and enemies, the learned and the politicians often predict its approaching death. But over the centuries it renews its requiems over these false seers of its doom.

Its flourishing life today shows that the Church does more than survive external attack and internal treason. She comes back from the cross, more full of life than she was before, more glorious than before. She comes back as Christ did, bearing the marks of old wounds, gracious to loyal followers, pitying her old enemies, and stronger with victories. The Bridegroom arisen never dies; neither does His holy Bride for whom He sacrificed Himself.

Therefore, we renew our faith at Easter in the risen Christ, in His holy Catholic Church, and in Peter who is Christ-on-earth. In a skeptical, troubled, cruel, and sin-spoiled world, how much it means to us to have the truth, the peace, the charity, and the joy of Peter. Having him, we have Christ. Having Peter, we have Christ's Bride as our Mother. *Ave, Sancta Mater Ecclesia.*

16. THE GRACE OF THE KING'S FESTIVAL

To My Father

On the happy morning of His resurrection, Rabbouni sent Mary Magdalene to His brethren with a special message: "By and by I will ascend to my Father and your Father, to my God and your God."[156] Perhaps He was harking back to His yearning remark at the Last Supper: "I have come from the Father and have come into the world. And now I am leaving the world and going home to the Father."[157] Home is where His Father is. The only normal place for His glorified body is with His glorious Father. His visible glorified body can linger only a little while longer on earth. Our needs, moreover, require Him to return homeward that He may send His Spirit and make ready our places by His side in heaven.

Some of our theologians believe that the risen Christ spent in heaven the intervals between His appearances on earth. The Ascension is the public final departure of the Saviour from the world He has saved. He seems to have held a farewell dinner with His followers, renewed His instructions about waiting for the Holy Spirit, and walked with them to Mount Olivet.[158]

Thence His body follows the craving of His soul to be with His Father. Inch by inch and slowly the Lord of Glory begins to rise from the ground. Presently His head tops the hair of the tallest disciples so that even those at the outer edges of the crowd see His face and shoulders rising in a gentle, bouyant movement. His countenance grows more radiant. His wounded right hand rises in glad blessing. His friends, spellbound by this new wonder, stare and stare. After some minutes the divine Eagle has soared so high that His human figure is but a quivering point of light. Finally, a cloud borne by angels sails by, and He is lost to their gaze.

Thereupon* He quickens His speed and now races, like a comet, to His Father's abode. Hosts of human souls, who have been waiting for centuries for this day, wing their way with Him after their release from limbo. Shining armies of angels come from heaven to escort Him; they and the guardian angels of the souls greet Him in mighty waves of song. The choruses of angels and saints answer each other's triumphant hosannas to their King.

* The next five paragraphs are not based on the Gospels and Acts.

Lift up your royal gates, and the Lord of glory will enter in.
  Who is this King of glory?
  He is the strong and mighty Lord of hosts.
Lift up your gate for the king's entrance;
  The Lord of glory is about to enter His own city.[159]

The advancing host, led by Christ, has reached the towering golden door of heaven. A special angel has guarded this door ever since Adam slammed shut the entrance to paradise. It has never been opened; no man, woman, or child has ever passed through it. But at the glance of the glorious Redeemer, the angel sheaths His sword, and the door springs open as though His eye electronically controls it. A joyous shout greets this token of the Victor's merit and power.

Jesus, standing before that opened gate, scarcely notices the surrounding heavenly beauties and treasures. His Heart is in His eyes, for the best sight of all, God Himself in His triune Infinity, beckons a welcome to His Son. Think of the sonorous wonder of God's voice ringing through every corner of that boundless heavenly land: "This is My beloved Son; in Him I am well pleased." Then God confers on the adoring human nature of His Son the first of many awards. "Son, wear this crown of the King of Kings, and sit at My right hand forever."

Next God turns His thought to the waiting saints. "Son, You have judged all these worthy of Our eternal company. Because You have saved them and they are dear to You, they are most welcome to be My children. I open the kingdom to all who know, hope in, and love You. Come, all; rejoice in the home of your Father."

Encouraged by His Father, the ascended Saviour then speaks for Himself and His redeemed brethren. "Glory be to You, My Father, today and forever. I love You because You are God, all good, and because You are My Father.

I accept this honor at Your right hand as another gift from You, knowing that it delights You to have Me accept it. My Father, I thank You for all You have done for Me, for helping Me suffer and die for these souls, and for raising Me from the grave and above the earth to be at home with You at last. Father, I have yearned for this day. I have looked forward to presenting the love of these My friends to You. Thank You for Your loving kindness to them."

Son of God and Son of Mary, King of heaven and of earth, we give You thanks for Your great glory.

THE OPENED GATE

We ought to let our hearts follow His ascending form and always keep an eye fixed on that cross-marked gate of triumph through which we must one day run into the divine presence. Our first entrance will be with cleansed souls after our penance in purgatory; our final entrance will follow the general resurrection when the beatified soul ushers in its own glorified body. We Catholics have scores of jokes about stealing into heaven by back doors and secret passages which the Virgin Mary opens for her little ones when St. Peter is not looking. But when we are theologically earnest, we know that no one enters except as a conquering hero and beloved son through the door which is Christ Himself.

He spoke of Himself as the Shepherd who watches the door through which only His own sheep enter. He also referred to Himself as the only Door. For through Him alone we get grace; through Him alone we can keep grace and win the eternal rewards due to the graced. "If one goes in through me, all will be well with him."[160] United with Christ in faith, charity, and the sacraments, we shall enter through His door; and we will repeat Magdalene's delighted cry: "I have seen [and see] the Lord."

All of us have a firm appointment to meet Jesus, first as our Judge at the moment of death and later as our Reward at the gate of heaven. On earth we must be busy fitting our souls for these meetings. One step in preparation is constant prayerful desire to see His and His Father's face. "Ask, and it shall be given to you; seek, and you shall find; knock, and it shall be opened to you."[161] God and heaven may be had for the asking if we ask in Christ's name and for the sake of His love.

Surely He will admit us through His door if on earth we welcome Him into our door. This mutual reception — of Christ into our souls and of our souls into Christ — is mentioned more than once in the doctrines on the Eucharist and charity. Perhaps its most vivid statement occurs in the Apocalypse: "Here I am standing at the door and knocking. If anyone listens to my call and opens the door, I will come to him and have supper with him and he with me. To him who is victorious, I will grant the favor of being seated beside me on my throne, as I too was victorious and am seated beside my Father on his throne."[162]

Come, then, Lord Jesus. Come in, take possession, and remain with us ever.

The Festival of Glory

What is this promised gift of heaven like? What kind of life do its citizens lead? These questions cannot be well answered on earth because our minds lack the capacity to understand the true answers until we see God and because human language, our human invention, is a clumsy tool for expressing these high truths. Yet Christ and the Holy Spirit have tried to help us appreciate heaven by giving us some glimpses of it. There seem to be four main pictures of heaven in Scripture. Heaven is payday and harvest-time for the workers of God. It is homecoming day for the orphaned children of God. It is the marriage feast celebrating the perpetual union of the Lamb with His Church and of God with each person's soul. It is the festival of glory for the victorious warriors of the risen King.

The most enthusiastic of these four pictures is the last, though not the most profound. St. John's imagery probably follows his memories of Roman imperial victory celebrations which he may have witnessed and must have heard about. The mid-century movie, *Quo Vadis?*, brilliantly reconstructed the triumph of the general Licinius.

John's visions of heaven foresaw the immense victory parade, led by the King of Kings mounted on His white horse.[163] His trophy is a place on the divine throne. He opens the scroll of His victories and in it, the book of life, He reads the names of all whom His great battle has redeemed. The wonderful City of Love and Peace is ablaze with the Lamb's self-luminous light. Its streets and homes are filled with the white-gowned saints and the gold-bright angels. And all of these raise new, joyous acclamations to the Lamb and King who has come through many perils to this day of glory. "Alleluia! The slain Lamb deserves to receive power and wealth and wisdom and strength and honor and glory and blessing." And the virgins whom He has kept pure have their own song as they follow the Lamb who has purchased for them a likeness to His virginity. "Blessed be Jesus Christ forever."

Triumphs for Roman generals and rulers usually came to a climax in a splendid feast with joyous entertainment, magnificent service, memorial addresses and toasts to the heroes, and awards for their legionaries. John, likewise, represents heaven as a feast of honor with Christ sharing His joy with His own in the new kingdom. This is the great dinner to which Christ has invited all members of His realm.[164] This is the eternal feast that was foreshadowed by the Jewish paschal meal and the Last Supper, and which is pledged in every Holy Communion, and to which the ecclesiastical celebrations of Easter, the Ascension, and All Saints' Day look forward. At this banquet Jesus shall drink with us the new wine of the kingdom of heaven,[165] and it shall inebriate us with the sweetness, the thanks, and the love of God. Angel choirs shall entertain us with the new music of heaven, sharing with us the glad fire of their spirits. Still mindful of each of us in the midst of His honors, Jesus shall speak to each with that new name which He finds for each one, a friend's own endearing name for his friend.[166]

That glorious banquet shall teach us what it is to be redeemed. For we prodigals have become princes of heaven since we are brothers of its King; we Cinderellas have left the sculleries of earth to be brides of the King of Heaven. There we shall feel all the happy ease of a family reunion without any of the hidden tension of ceremonial state dinners. One of the exciting gifts to be presented at this celestial banquet is the unfading laurel of glory which the divine Prince gives to each who has worn His crown of thorns on earth's little calvaries.

But human images fall to pieces in the attempt to catch a preview of heaven. Eye has not seen, ear has not heard, the heart of man cannot rightly conceive what joys God has prepared for those who love Him.[167] But if the glimpse be so sparkling, what must be the vision; if the sip be so sweet, what must be the feast!

Every meal on earth taken with right intentions should quicken our desire for the everlasting feast with Christ and our brethren. Every Host at the Eucharistic table prepares us better for our place at the eternal table of the Lord where every hunger of the spirit shall be filled. The monastic grace at table closes with a yearning aspiration, "May the King of eternal glory make us sharers in His heavenly feast."

Our most jubilant alleluias at Easter time sound like long sighs for that unfading morning with the beloved Blessed Trinity.

The simple old prayer, *Anima Christi*, says it for us very well: "Good Jesus, in the hour of my death call for me, and order me to come to You, that with Your saints I may forever praise You. Amen."

Indeed, Amen! In our Father's house every day will be Happy Easter.

17. THE GRACE OF THE PROMISED SPIRIT

THE PLEDGE OF ANOTHER COMFORTER

The season of the Resurrection comes to its joyful climax in the coming of the Holy Spirit on Pentecost. This arrival fully carries out Christ's solemn, repeated pledge that He would send His own Spirit for our comforting. Jesus had enjoyed the constant companionship of the Third Person of God during His own life on earth. He knew that our life in Christ would be very incomplete without this

same loving Person abiding with us. So, He sent Him
as His supreme paschal gift.

Our Lord told us both who the Spirit is and what He
is to do for us. He is the third in order within the Blessed
Trinity, proceeding from both the Father and the Son, as
fully divine as They are, as holy as They are, one with
Them in loving will. He is the Bond, the Kiss of love, the
Embrace that ties the Father to the Son. He acts not only
within God but also within the whole of creation and the
whole world of grace, wherever the Father and Son act.
When God loves us, the Spirit loves us. He is the Spirit
of Truth, the Teacher who unites wisdom with love.
Divinely commissioned to come to the Church as the
Spirit of Christ, He teaches all that He has heard from
the Second Person. He is the friendly helper of the
Church's teachers until the end of time. As the Spirit of
Holiness, He distributes all graces whereby men conquer
sin and grow in perfection.

Our Lord especially describes Him as a second Advocate
or Comforter.[168] He is an advocate in the old legal sense
of a helper to those in need and a counselor to those in
doubt. As comforter, He befriends men in their troubles
by protecting them in spiritual danger and easing their
anxious sorrows. He is another Comforter in addition to
Christ. He comforts by teaching, forgiving, empowering,
and loving. To call Him the Comforter in a way sums up
all His works. Moreover, He comes to us, never alone but
together with the Father and the Son, so that Christ in
His divine nature returns to us whenever the Holy Spirit
is a guest dwelling in us, His palaces.

The heavenly Spirit had been busy in the world long
before Pentecost. He had breathed life into the universe
and into Adam's body. He had spoken through the prophets.[169] He had assisted the virginal conception of the Christ

Child.[170] He had been seen as a dove hovering over Christ in the Jordan. He had come upon the Apostles at their ordination the night before Calvary. On Easter morning He was present in the grave where His divine power restored life to the martyred body of Christ. Some believe that the Church is recalling His part in the Resurrection when she blesses the new fire on Easter eve.[171] The flint represents the dead Christ in the rocky tomb; the spark struck is the Spirit; the fire is Christ's risen life, lit by the Spirit's warm might. Thus, the Spirit's bright love had shed splendor on the body of Christ, working the miracle of the Resurrection to show that God accepts Christ's sacrifice on the cross.

At His first general visit with His Apostles on Easter evening, Christ deepened their share in His Spirit. He breathed on them — such breathing is a sign of the movement of the living spirit — and gave them the Spirit with the power to pardon sins.[172] As His ambassadors, they needed sanctifying powers as well as teaching powers. They were soon ordered to enroll converts who had heard the Spirit's message and to give them sanctifying grace through the rite of baptism.[173] Till the end of time, the Spirit is imparted to each Christian; and each is consecrated to the Spirit by the holy words: "I baptize you in the name of the Father and of the Son and of the Holy Spirit." Baptism itself is crowned by the second coming of the Spirit in the sacrament of confirmation.

Our Lord knew that, left to themselves, the Apostles would forget some of His teachings, misunderstand some doctrines as they had done while He lived among them, grow confused by doctrinal attacks, and lose heart in their immense missionary task of spreading His name and truth over the whole world. But their inabilities did not trouble Him. He would send the Spirit of Truth to remind them of all truths, to rectify their misconceptions, and to strengthen them in bearing their burden as His witnesses. Christ had serene confidence in the gracious, fruitful Missionary whom He was sending with all His love.

Accordingly, His final instructions to them required them to spend nine prayerful days in pleading and waiting for the outpouring of Christ's best gift to them.[174]

THE DIVINE WIND BLOWS

Nine days after His enthronement at the Father's right hand, Jesus keeps His promise to send His Spirit to His little Church. This time the Spirit does not appear as a divine bird sailing on a down draft from heaven. He comes in a blowing rush of wind. He rests on the heads of Mary and the Apostles in the visible sign of fiery parted tongues, which show that each has received the Spirit and the one same Spirit of Christ.[175]

Wind and tongues aptly represent the Spirit's place in their lives. Air, being invisible, energetic, and needful for life, is a very old symbol for spirit and life. The breathing of air marks the presence of the living soul and its control over the body of man. The movement of air is also likened to the reaching out of the lover going to his beloved. The yearning sigh, the gasp of delight are uses of breath that externalize the movements of lovers' hearts and wills.[176] The swirling wind showed the strength of the Spirit, therefore, and His delight in coming, and His life-giving presence. The strangeness of this special wind in this special spot in the city drew crowds to the site.

The fiery divided tongues speak, of course, of the Teacher of Truth who has settled on the minds of these human ambassadors of Christ. These fire-bright tongues flash with light, flare with energy, leap with love. Their redness tells us, too, by its symbolism of courage and love, that in Christ's religion learning and a martyr's fidelity to truth must go together. The many tongues give them power, without further study of languages, to instruct all nations. Indeed, Peter's audience that day hear him in at least fifteen languages. The same gift of being understood by all who heard them is thought to have accompanied all the Apostles in their later missionary enterprises.

The coming of this Third divine Person on Pentecost, which is known as the visible, external, social mission of the Holy Spirit, is meant more for the help of souls and the upbuilding of the Church than for the personal holiness of the Twelve. The power of the Gift appears in the astonishing first sermon that same morning when Peter addresses the milling crowds.[177] To these Jews he fearlessly proclaims the Resurrection of Christ recently crucified by their leaders. He interprets the profound prophecies of Joel about the coming of the Spirit and applies it to today's wind. He explains David's words about the divinity and rising of Christ. He gives witness, as one authorized to announce truth, to the Spirit who has filled him and his associates. Men so disheartened seven weeks ago are today so bold? Unschooled men, today so wise? Backward provincials, today masters of many languages? Common fishermen turned into ambassadors of the King of Heaven? The towering thinking in the apostolic preaching is itself a creation of the Spirit, not of the minds of men.

Peter, furthermore, assured all who were willing to be baptized that the Holy Spirit would come also upon them. Three thousand converts accepted Christ's religion that day.

Since the feast of Pentecost commemorates the public mission of the Comforter, the liturgy is primarily directed to the coming of the Spirit to the officials and new con-

verts of the Church. Our prayers beg that the initial gift
to the Church may continue as a perpetual presence of
the Spirit of Christ in us, His mystical body. We address
our Father and our Saviour:

Send forth Thy Spirit, and our earth shall be renewed.[178]

Next we plead with the Spirit directly:

Come, fill the hearts of the faithful.
Come, set love burning in our hearts.

The seasonal prayers ask light for the whole Church, and
cleansing of the soul, right desires, comfort and consolation, peace and joy, protection, full wisdom, fervor and
fruitfulness, unity of the Church, and love, the greatest
blessing of all. The Collect of Pentecost Sunday makes the
most appealing of these many requests:

O God, who this very day taught the hearts of the faithful by
the radiant light of Your Holy Spirit,
bless us with these gifts:
a relish for what is good and lasting joy in Your comforting.

Among the effects of the external mission of the Spirit
of Love must be included the whole life of the Church
and the great glory of Christ on earth.

GIFTS FROM THE DIVINE GIFT

Besides this public outpouring, the heavenly Spirit
gently descends into individual souls for their sanctifica-
tion. This invisible personal mission was also prayed for
and merited for us by Christ. By the continuing visits of
Christ's Spirit the soul becomes gradually richer in grace.
He makes His first loving entrance into a child's soul in
baptism; again in confirmation; later with His pardon in
penance; in Holy Communion when He accompanies
Christ; in the hour of our wedding; and in the last sacra-

ment. Whenever He comes with His gift of sanctifying grace, He the Donor comes, personally bearing His gifts and remaining with us as long as we allow.

He is well named the Gift,[179] for gifts are the lover's way of life. Love loves to give. Christ in heaven loves to send this Gift to us. The Gift rejoices exceedingly to come with His many spiritual blessings. Besides Himself and sanctifying grace, these favors include the virtues faith, hope, charity, and other supernatural habits; His seven special gifts; and countless actual graces for our minds and wills. To His generosity must also be credited those specially finished acts of the soul which we know as the fruits of the Holy Spirit. Our peace, joy, keen faith, and warm love at the Easter season are instances of such fruits which the living Spirit within us produces.

We would have to write rather detailed autobiographies if we were to number or mention all the actual graces with which the Spirit has enlightened and enheartened each of us. We depend on Him for all of these and are most grateful for them. Two great chains of these actual graces deserve our special thanksgiving: the grace of our accepted vocation in the Christian life and the grace of final perseverance. We trust His never-ending love to keep on linking these graces until we see Him in heaven.

Like an extravagant lover, the Gift wills to pour upon us far more graces than we are altogether eager to receive. But if we would have them, He would press His favors on us. He is the Comforter, ever standing by to help us in this life. He is God, waiting for our coming to Himself and the Father and the Son when He may heap on us the blessed love of heaven which we merit by good use of His graces. His liberality has no limit.

Moreover, He is faithful in His love. Once sent to the Church, He has never deserted her. Once received into our souls, this holy Visitor will never leave us unless our free wills force Him to go forth. In spite of our immeasurable needs for Him, our self-love can block His coming and can reject His selfless love. To be faithful in our love of Him, we need more and more of His visits and gifts; fidelity is also His gift to us.

Christ and His Church often urge us to open our hearts and wills to this Spirit, to pray for Him insistently, to welcome Him, to respond to His love and cherish His gifts, and to hold Him fast within our souls at all times.

"Come. Come. Veni. Ever welcome. Come and stay." So many hymns and prayers to the Holy Spirit begin with this invitation. The heavenly Dove is ready to wing His way to us as soon as He knows we truly want Him. To perfect our welcome, we address Him by all those endearing names which Christ ascribed to Him. Come, Spirit of Truth, Advocate and Comforter, our second Paraclete. Come, Spirit of Christ. Come, Spirit of Love. Come, Teacher of Christ's doctrines. Come, Spirit of Forgiveness.

We coax His visits also by the fond names which the Apostles and the Church suggest. Come, creative Spirit. Come, Holy Spirit. Come, gift-laden Gift of God. Come, Fire of Charity. Come, Father of the poor who so need Your grace. Come, sweet Guest of the Soul. Come, Anointer and consecrating Ointment touching the spirit. Come, Promise of the Father and the Son. Come; Finger of the Father. Come, Artist beautifying the souls of the Father's children. Come, come, Light of Minds and Hearts.[180]

Come, most holy Spirit, at your own good pleasure. Shape our souls for Your descent into us. Come with what gifts Your own love suggests that You bring. Give us Yourself and Your love, for he who has God's love has everything.

Mary, our Mother and Bride of the Holy Spirit, when you pray that we may be worthy of the promises of Christ, remember to pray above all that we may worthily receive the greatest Promise, the Holy Spirit to be sent by Christ your Son.

Risen Saviour, we know You are most true to Your promises. From Your throne, then, near our Father, "pour forth the Spirit of Your Love into our hearts so that, after You have filled us with Your Easter sacraments, the action of Your brotherly love may make us men of one heart."[181]

NOTES AND REFERENCES

Introduction

1. The sequence and concordance of Christ's apparitions have often been studied. Cf. St. Augustine, *De Consensu Evangelistarum*, III, Chap. 25 (*Patrologia Latina*, 34:214); C. Lattey, S.J., "The Apparitions of the Risen Christ," *Catholic Biblical Quarterly*, July, 1940, 105–214; G. Ricciotti, *The Life of Christ*, translated by A. I. Zizzamia (Milwaukee: Bruce, 1947), unabridged edition, third printing, Chap. 26.
2. *The New Testament*, translated by James A. Kleist, S.J. (the Gospels) and Joseph L. Lilly, C.M. (Epistles and Apocalypse) (Milwaukee: Bruce, 1954).

1. The Grace of the Risen Body, pages 1–7

3. Cf. Apoc. 22:16 where Christ uses this name of Himself. Zachary used it in the *Benedictus*. The Church uses it in the Easter chant, the *Exultet*.
4. Introit of Mass of Easter Sunday, drawn from Ps. 138:18.
5. Cf. Jn. 17:1, 5.
6. St. Teresa of Avila, *Life of St. Teresa of Jesus by Herself*, translated by David Lewis (London: Thomas Baker, 1924), 5th ed., Chap. 28, sec. 7.
7. St. Thomas Aquinas, *Summa Theologiae*, III, q. 54. The Ottawa edition, 1941–1944, has been used throughout.
8. In the Gradual of all Masses of Easter week, taken from Ps. 117:24. Psalm 117 is known as the Easter psalm because of frequent excerpts in the liturgy of this season.
9. Col. 1:18; cf. Apoc. 1:5.
10. 1 Cor. 15:20–23.
11. Cf. Rom. 9:28–30; Phil. 3:20–21; St. Thomas Aquinas, *Summa Theologiae*, III, q. 56, a. 1, ad 1, 3, 4 for texts on conformity to Christ; *Summa contra Gentiles*, IV, Chap. 82–86, 88 for properties of glorified bodies.
12. 1 Cor. 15:35, 42–43; cf. Thess. 4:14, 16.
13. Col. 3:4.
14. Cf. Job 19:25–27. This is the first of the great acts of faith in the bodily resurrection of the good.
15. Cf. Jn. 11:25, the raising of Lazarus.
16. Cf. Jn. 6:54–55, 58.

2. The Grace of His Wounds, pages 8–14

17. Jn. 20:27.
18. Cf. *Summa Theologiae*, III, q. 54, a. 4.
19. Cf. *Roman Missal*, Preface of Mass of the Sacred Heart.
20. Cf. Hebr. 8:5; 13:13.
21. Cf. Acts 5:41; Col. 1:24; Phil. 3:10–11.
22. Cf. *Roman Missal*, Collect of the Mass of the Sacred Heart.
23. Cf. *Sainte Marguerite Marie: La Vie Écrite par elle-même* (Paris: Editions Saint-Paul, 1947), pp. 70–71 and 60. Clarence A. Herbst, S.J., *Letters of Saint Margaret Mary Alacoque*, translated (Chicago: Regnery, 1954), has many passages on reparation.
24. Cf. E. C. E. Owens, translator, *Some Authentic Acts of the Early Martyrs* (Oxford: Clarendon Press, 1927), p. 91.
25. "*Salvete, Christi Vulnera*," by an unknown author in the seventeenth century. The hymn beginning with these lines is used at Lauds on the Feast of the Most Precious Blood, July 1.

3. The Grace of a Visit With Mary, pages 15–21

26. Sister M. Madeleva, C.S.C., *Collected Poems* (New York: Macmillan, 1947), p. 91, "Of Wounds" presents Mary viewing His glorified body.
27. Cf. Herbert Thurston, S.J., *Familiar Prayers, their Origin and History* (Westminster, Md.: Newman, 1953), 146–151.

4. The Grace of the Paschal Lamb, pages 22–29

28. Cf. Exod. Chapters 12–14; Clifford Howell, S.J., *Preparing for Easter* (Collegeville: Liturgical Press, 1955), passim.
29. Cf. Lev. 7:15, 23:5; Num. 9:12, 28:16.
30. The phrase is from 1 Cor. 5:7.
31. Jn. 1:29.
32. Cf. Apoc. Chapters 5, 7, 19, 21. The priest uses these words when facing the people before their communicating; hence, it is a festive symbol for First Communion.
33. Cf. definition of the Council of Trent in H. Denzinger, *Enchiridion Symbolorum*, 29th edition by C. Rahner, S.J. (Freiburg im Breisgau: Herder, 1953), no. 875; cf. 1 Cor. 11:24.
34. A prose translation of "*Victimae Paschali Laudes*." Karl Young in *The Drama of the Medieval Church* (Oxford: Clarendon Press, 1933), Vol. I, discusses at length the use of this hymn and play up to the sixteenth century.
35. Apoc. 5:12.
36. A thought drawn from St. Thomas' "*Adoro Te Devote*." There is a smooth translation by Gerard Manley Hopkins.
37. It is customary to list seven bloodsheddings: the circumcision, agony, scourging, crowning with thorns, way of the cross, crucifixion, and piercing of Christ's Heart. Cf. Frederick W. Faber, *The Precious*

Blood (Baltimore: John Murphy, n.d.), Chap. 5, pp. 260 ff.

38. We find some musicians preferring the Agnus Dei to the Credo as a favorite Easter piece. Easter radio programs often feature the Agnus Dei from *Cavalleria Rusticana*.

39. Cf. St. Gregory the Great, *Dialogues*, IV, 59 (*Patrologia Latina*, LXXVII, 428). The same thought is in the charge of the ordaining bishop to the candidates for the priesthood during the Mass of ordinations: "*Imitamini quod agitis*."

5. The Grace of the Second Life, pages 30–36

40. Cf. Rom. 6:9.
41. Apoc. 1:18; cf. 2:8.
42. The Latin text of "*Victimae Paschali Laudes*" here runs:
    Mors et vita duello conflixere mirando
    Dux vitae mortuus regnat vivus.
43. Cf. St. Thomas Aquinas, *Summa Theologiae*, III, q. 49, a. 3 ad 1, 3.
44. Cf. Jn. 11:25; 1:4.
45. Cf. Jn. 10:17–18; 1 Jn. 1:2; Jn. 1:16.
46. Col. 2:12–14.
47. Rom. 6:3–7.
48. See the ending of the ceremony of baptism in *Collectio Rituum* (Milwaukee: Bruce, 1954), pp. 17–18. The rising from the tomb explains the grace of supernatural life and of baptism by a set of images that differ from the more familiar series associated with the concepts of being born again, of the womb of Mother Church, godparents, etc. Sometimes the Church uses one and sometimes the other series and sometimes skips from one to the other.
49. Cf. Col. 3:1–15; much of Chapters 1 and 2 of this Epistle is to be read in the same sense; cf. Rom. 6:6–14; Eph. 2:4–9; Gal. 5:13–28; 1 Pet. 1:15–16, 22–23; 2:1–12; 3:8–12; 2 Pet. 1:5–12; 2:20–21.
50. 1 Pet. 2:9; cf. 1 Cor. 12:27.

6. The Grace of Forgiveness, pages 37–43

51. Jn. 20:19; Lk. 24:36.
52. Cf. Jn. 20:19 ff.; Lk. 24:34 ff.; Mk. 16:14.
53. Cf. Jn. 20:19; Lk. 24:36.
54. Jn. 20:21 ff.
55. Lk. 24:47.
56. Cf. Jn. 16:8–11.
57. Cf. Eph. 2:4–5.
58. Cf. Col. 3:14.

7. The Grace of Heavenly Desires, pages 44–50

59. Cf. Mt. 28:5–7 and Mk. 16:6–7.
60. Lk. 11:9.

61. See *The Roman Missal:* in paschal-vigil ceremonies: the blessing of the new fire, prayer after the first prophecy, the petition for minds lifted to desire heavenly things near end of the litany of the saints; Collect of third Sunday after Pentecost; Collect and Secret of fourth Sunday after Pentecost; Collect and Postcommunion of fifth Sunday after Pentecost.

62. Cf. Collect of the feast of our Lord's Ascension.

63. Cf. last prayer before the start of the Mass of the Vigil of Pentecost.

64. Cf. Col. 3:3.

65. Cf. Rom. 8:26 and certain petitions of the Our Father.

66. The connection of the Resurrection and renunciation is found in Col. 3:5 ff. and Rom. 6:5 ff. Detachment is a capital point in the spiritual doctrine of both St. Ignatius Loyola and St. John of the Cross.

67. Cf. Alexandre Brou, S.J., *The Ignatian Way to God*, translated by William J. Young, S.J. (Milwaukee: Bruce, 1952), p. 91; *Autobiography of St. Thérèse of Lisieux*, where we read that the first word she learned to read was the French for heaven.

68. Col. 3:4.

8. The Grace of the Victor's Crown, pages 51–59

69. Francis Thompson, "The Veteran of Heaven," third stanza, in *The Works of Francis Thompson* (New York: Scribner's, 1913), edited by Wilfred Meynell, I, pp. 149–150; also reprinted in various anthologies.

70. Cf. 1 Cor. 15:54–55.

71. Cf. Apoc. 17:14 and Ps. 2:2, 4.

72. Cf. Phil. 2:9–10.

73. Cf. Jn. 17:4–5.

74. Cf. Jn. 12:32–33.

75. The translation of these lines is by J. M. Neale. Cf. Matthew Britt, O.S.B., *The Hymns of the Breviary and the Missal* (New York: Benziger, 1922), p. 126. Quoted with permission.

76. 2 Tim. 10–12; cf. Rom. 8:17; 1 Pet. 4:13.

77. Apoc. 2:10; cf. *id.* 2:17, 27–28.

9. The Grace of Faith, pages 60–68

78. Cf. Mt. 16:15–16.

79. Cf. Jn. 20:8.

80. Cf. Jn. 20:24–29; St. Thomas Aquinas, *Summa Theologiae*, III, q. 55, a. 5, obj. 3 and ad 3.

81. Cf. Jn. 11:16.

82. Jn. 20:27–29. Several lines are taken from the translation by David Michael Stanley, S.J., in "St. John and the Paschal Mystery," *Worship*, April, 1959 (33), pp. 293 ff.

83. The doctrine on faith is drawn from the Councils, Trent and Vati-

can. Cf. H. Denzinger, *Enchiridion Symbolorum*, 29th edition by C. Rahner, S.J. (Freiburg im Breisgau: Herder, 1953), nos. 797, 799, 801, 814; and 1789, 1791, 1811, 1814.
84. Cf. Acts 9:1–19.
85. Cf. Jn. 17:20.
86. Cf. Phil. 2:17.
87. Cf. Mt. Chapter 5.
88. Jn. 6:47; cf. Jn. 3:14–16, 36; 5:25; 6:40.
89. Cf. 1 Pet. 1:8–9; St. Paul's similar statement in Rom. 1:16–17; 3:22; 10:9–10; 1 Tim. Chapters 1–16.
90. Cf. Jn. 20:31.
91. 1 Jn. 5:5–6, 13.
92. *Collectio Rituum* (Milwaukee: Bruce, 1954), p. 4 and pp. 10–11. Blessings of baptismal font and baptismal water occur on the Easter Vigil, cf. *Roman Missal*.
93. *"Lumen Christi,"* i.e., Light of Christ.
94. 2 Tim. 4:7.

10. The Grace of Christ's Friendship, pages 69–75

95. "My brethren," in Mt. 28:10; Jn. 20:17.
96. Cf. St. Thomas Aquinas, *Summa Theologiae*, III, q. 55, aa. 1, 3.
97. Cf. Jn. 16:20, 22, 24; 15:11; 17:13; Mt. 5:10–12; 16:27; Lk. 18:28–30.
98. *Summa Theologiae*, III, q. 55, a. 3 contends that the double purpose of Christ's manifestation is to give evidence of the fact of the Resurrection and the glory of the risen One.
99. 1 Cor. 9:22 Caryll Houselander, *The Risen Christ* (New York: Sheed and Ward, 1958), pp. 36–44, has some interesting guesses on this theme of personal differences.
100. Eph. 3:14–19; cf. 2 Cor. 4:6.
101. Cf. Jn. 14:15; 15:10; 1 Jn. 4:12, 16; 5:3.
102. 2 Cor. 5:15.
103. Cf. Apoc. 20:4; 2 Cor. 7:3; Phil. 3:10–11; Gal. 2:20; 2 Tim. 2:11–13.
104. The series of expressions occurs in Jn. 20:16, 19; 21:7, 15–17; Lk. 24:29; Apoc. 22:17, 21.
105. Cf. Clarence A. Herbst, S.J., *Letters of Saint Margaret Mary Alacoque* (Chicago: Regnery, 1954), translated, p. 268; cf. 202 ff., 223. The texts concern the promise of the Sacred Heart's fidelity in the hour of death.

11. The Grace of Divine Care, pages 76–83

106. Cf. Lk. 24:26 and 45; Mk. 16:12–13.
107. See especially Psalms 21 (quoted on the Cross), 68, 15; Isa. Chapters 50, 53; Mal. 1:11; Zach. 9:9–10; 11:10–12; 12:10.
108. The phrase comes from the Preface of the Cross: *"Qui in ligno*

vincebat in ligno quoque vinceretur." Bl. Jacopo de Voragine in
The Golden Legends writes of the numerical identity of the wood
in Paradise and on Calvary; and this legend appears in Piero della
Francesca's famous paintings on The True Cross.

109. Mt. 5:10–12; the parallel in Lk. 6:22–23.
110. Cf. Mt. 16:25; Mk. 8:35; Lk. 17:33; Jn. 12:24–25. The text on
the lilies is Lk. 12:27; cf. Mt. 6:28–29.
111. Cf. Mt. 16:24; Mk. 8:34; Lk. 14:27, 33.
112. For Paul: cf. Rom. 8:17; 2 Cor. 4:10; 5:15; Col. 1:24; Gal. 2:19–
20; 6:14; Phil. 2:5–11; 3:10–11. For Peter: cf. Acts 5:41; 1 Pet.
2:21; 4:13–14, 19. Two celebrated chapters of The Imitation of
Christ treat the same theme: cf. II, Chap. 11–12.
113. The Epistle of "Good Shepherd Sunday" is read from 1 Pet. 2:21–
25; the Gospel from Jn. 10:11–16. Cf. Hebr. 13:20 on the Shepherd back from His death.
114. Cf. Ps. 22.
115. Cf. Ps. 70:1. It also closes the Te Deum.

12. The Grace of a Garden, pages 84–90

116. Cf. Jn. 19:41.
117. Cf. Lk. 22:43 and Apoc. 22:2, 40.
118. 2 Cor. 4:4–6.
119. Cf. Jn. 20:1, 11–18; Mt. 28:1–10; Mk. 16:9–11; Lk. 24:11.
120. Cf. 2 Cor. 2:14–16.
121. Cf. Apoc. 22:2, 20.

13. The Grace of Signs, pages 91–98

122. Mt. 12:38–40; cf. Lk. 11:29–32; Jonas 1:12–16; 2:1–11.
123. Cf. Mt. 16:4; Lk. 11:6.
124. Cf. Jn. 2:13–22; other prophecies of His Resurrection in Mt. 20:17–
20; Lk. 18:33.
125. Cf. Mt. 27:39–43; Mk. 15:29–32; Lk. 23:35–39.
126. Cf. Mt. 28:5–7; Mk. 16:5–8; Lk. 24:1–7.
127. Karl Young, The Drama of the Early Medieval Church (Oxford:
Clarendon Press, 1933), I, pp. 267 and 318.
128. Cf. doctrine of the Angelic Doctor on the Resurrection as sign
in Summa Theologiae, III, q. 56, aa. 5, 6 and q. 44, a. 3.
129. Cf. Lk. 24:41–42.
130. Cf. Jn. 21:1 ff.
131. Cf. George Ferguson, Signs and Symbols in Christian Art (New
York: Oxford University Press, 1955), 2nd ed., Section I; Louis
Réau, Iconographie de L'Art Chrétienne (Paris: Presses Universi-
taires, 1955), I, 81, 83, 88, 96.
132. André Pelletier, S.J., "The rending of the temple veil," Theology
Digest, spring, 1959, p. 127.
133. Cf. Mt. 24:30.

134. Cf. Mk. 16:20. The doctrine of the Vatican Council on miracles as signs is in nos. 1794, 1812, 1813 of H. Denzinger, *Enchiridion Symbolorum* (Freiburg im Breisgau: Herder, 1953), 29th ed. by C. Rahner, S.J.
135. Cf. Our Lord's discourses in Mt. 25:31–46 and Jn. 15:12–17; also 1 Jn., chap. 2–4 and 5:2; 2 Jn. 4:6; 3 Jn. 5; 1 Cor. 13.

14. The Grace of Witnessing, pages 99–105

136. Lk. 24:18; cf. Acts 1:8.
137. Lk. 24:39 in Rheims version. The analysis of aspects of the evidence follows *Summa Theologiae*, III, q. 56, a. 6, c.
138. Jn. 20:21; cf. Jn. 5:20; 15:27; 17:18–19.
139. Cf. Mt. 28:19–20.
140. Cf. Rom. 10:17; 1 Cor. 11:10.
141. Acts 2:37; cf. 10:33.
142. Jn. 13:20; Mt. 10:40; Lk. 10:16.
143. Gal. 4:14.
144. Cf. Mt. 10:33; Lk. 6:22–23; 12:8–9.

15. The Grace of the Rock and the Shepherd, pages 106–112

145. Cf. Mt. 7:24–25; Lk. 6:47–49.
146. Cf. Mt. 21:42–44; Lk. 20:17. The famous set of texts on the cornerstone includes Ps. 117:22–23; Isa. 28:16; Acts 4:11–12; Rom. 9:33; 1 Pet. 2:4–8. "The rock was Christ," in 1 Cor. 10:4. Cognate texts on the church as a building: 1 Cor. 3:10–14; 1 Tim. 3:15.
147. Cf. Mt. 16:13–20; Mk. 8:27–30; Lk. 9:18–20.
148. Cf. Jn. 20:2–10.
149. Cf. Lk. 24:35.
150. Cf. Lk. 22:32.
151. The Vatican Council's teaching on the perpetuity of the papacy by Christ's intention is reported in H. Denzinger, *Enchiridion Symbolorum* (Freiburg im Breisgau: Herder, 1953), 29th ed. by C. Rahner, S.J., nos. 1824–1825.
152. Cf. Jn. 21:1–19.
153. Cf. Jn. 10:11–18.
154. Cf. Jn. 6:33–35, 48–58. This discourse ends with Peter's declaration of faith in the Holy Eucharist: cf. Jn. 6:68–69.
155. Cf. Mt. 16:18; 24:35; 28:20; Mk. 13:31; Lk. 21:33; 22:32.

16. The Grace of the King's Festival, pages 113–120

156. Jn. 21:17.
157. Jn. 16:28.
158. Cf. Acts 1:1–12.
159. Cf. Ps. 23:7–10.
160. Jn. 10:9.
161. Mt. 7:7–8; Lk. 11:9–10 (Rheims version); cf. Jn. 14:13–14.

162. Apoc. 3:20–21.
163. Most of these images are taken from this series of texts in the Apocalypse: 15:11 ff.; chap. 5; 2:5–6 and 21:23 and 22:5; 7:9–17; 14:2–4. There are five or more related texts elsewhere in this book of St. John. The acclamation quoted is from Apoc. 5:12; other acclamations occur in 4:8, 11; 14:2–4; 19:2, 5–7; 1 Tim. 6:15–16; Jude 2.
164. Cf. Lk. 14:15 ff.; 13:19–20.
165. Cf. Lk. 22:18.
166. Cf. Apoc. 2:17; 3:12.
167. Cf. 1 Cor. 2:9; Isa. 64:4; Jer. 3:6.

17. The Grace of the Promised Spirit, pages 121–129

168. Cf. Jn. 14:16–18, 25–26; 15:26–27; 16:5–14; Joel 2:23–32 which is used by St. Peter in his Pentecostal sermon: Acts 2:16–21.
169. Cf. Acts 1:16. This idea occurs in the Nicene Creed, which is recited at Mass.
170. Cf. Lk. 1:35 and the phrase of the Apostles' Creed: "Who was conceived by the Holy Spirit."
171. Cf. Thomas O'Neill, S.J., "The New Fire," Worship, April, 1958 (32), 268–280.
172. Cf. Jn. 20:23.
173. Cf. Mt. 28:19–20; Jn. 3:5–8 (conversation with Nicodemus).
174. Cf. Acts 1:4–5; Lk. 24:49.
175. Cf. Acts 2:1–11.
176. St. Thomas Aquinas, Summa Theologiae, I, q. 36, a. 1 on the symbolism of air and tongues.
177. Cf. Acts 2:14–33.
178. Cf. Ps. 103:30.
179. On Gift as a name of the Holy Spirit, see Summa Theologiae, I, q. 38.
180. "Veni, Sancte Spiritus" is the sequence in Masses of Pentecost week. The more stately "Veni, Creator Spiritus" is used liturgically at Terce during Pentecost week and as a processional and invocation in many ceremonies. Translations of both are given in Matthew Britt, O.S.B., Hymns of the Breviary and Missal (New York: Benziger, 1922).
181. Cf. daily Postcommunion of the triduum from the eve of Easter to Easter Monday.